MORE LIES ABOUT LEARNING

Leading Executives Separate
Truth From Fiction

PRESS

Larry Israelite, Editor

ATD Press is an internationally renowned source of insightful and practical information on
talent development, workplace learning, and professional development.

ATD Press
1640 King Street
Alexandria, VA 22314 USA

Ordering information: Books published by ATD Press can be purchased by visiting ATD's
website at www.td.org/books or by calling 800.628.2783 or 703.683.8100.

Library of Congress Control Number: 2015934787

ISBN-10: 1-56286-949-3
ISBN-13: 978-1-56286-949-6
e-ISBN: 978-1-60728-276-1

ATD Press Editorial Staff
Director: Kristine Luecker
Manager: Christian Green
Community of Practice Manager, Learning & Development: Amanda Smith
Editors: Jack Harlow and Melissa Jones
Text Layout & Design: Bey Bello
Cover Design: Marisa Fritz and Maggie Hyde

Printed by Versa Press, Inc., East Peoria, IL, www.versapress.com

Contents

Part IV: Wrap-Up

Preface

My friends and family asked me why I would want to work on this book again. "After all," they said, "you've done this once already. How many more lies can there be? And if there are new lies, can they possibly be all that different from the lies you covered in the first edition?" Sadly, the answer is yes. While most—though not all—of the topics are the same, the lies are often different, and even when the lies are the same, the technologies about which they are being told are different. Regardless, it is the fact that so much has changed in the past nine years, while so much has seemingly remained the same, that made this project so appealing.

Lies About Learning was published in September 2006. A Bush was president, an actor governed California, and the world economy was about to begin its long, slow descent into oblivion. We were not yet consumed with the idea of multiple generations in the workplace (although there were). Being mobile meant you and your family were able to relocate. And social collaboration meant that people actually talked to one other, usually face to face. It was a different time. As learning leaders, our jobs have become more complex, largely because of economic pressure, fewer choices, and a loss of control. The first two are easy to describe; the last is a little less so.

Economic Pressure

While some might say that the economy has improved, I think we can safely say things haven't returned to the way they were. There is what I have heard referred to as a "new normal." There is a heightened interest in efficiency: How can we deliver solutions that cost less, take less time to produce, and require less time away from the job? Effectiveness matters more than ever, although that's not to say that it didn't matter before. It's just that demonstrating that learning has actually occurred—and that this learning has transferred to work performance—has become more important than it might have been earlier. And learning leaders feel constant pressure to make every decision and every dollar yield results that benefit the organization.

Fewer Choices

In late 2007, I sought a learning management system with features that supported talent management. Among others, I gave serious consideration to partnering with KnowledgePlanet, Learn.com, and Plateau Systems, all of which are different today than they were then. KnowledgePlanet merged with Mzinga. Learn.com was purchased by Taleo, which was then purchased by Oracle. And Plateau Systems was purchased by Success-Factors, which was subsequently purchased by SAP. Another example is a company from which I used to buy technical competency models. That company was purchased by Salary.com, which was purchased by Kenexa, which was purchased by IBM. Some days it seems as though I am a character in a Russian novel. The result is that if I were buying the same technologies today, I would be dealing with Oracle, SAP, and IBM, which is very different than in 2007.

Is it bad that some of the largest players in the industry have decided that talent was a space worthy of investment? Honestly, I'm not sure. But some of the most innovative products and services come from lean, hungry, and flexible companies. And there seem to be fewer of them left. Those that do remain are sometimes hidden in the very long shadow of much larger companies that have a direct pipeline to very influential people inside corporate walls.

Loss of Control

While not always the case, we used to control our own destiny with regard to the tools and technologies at our disposal. Sure, we rarely got to choose whether to use PCs or Macs, and I doubt that any of us were consulted when our employers embraced Microsoft Office as the office productivity suite. But we did get to choose our authoring tools, graphics editor, or virtual learning platforms, as long as the output conformed to some standards or technologies within a company's technical infrastructure. My concern is that this may be changing.

Technologies that existed solely (or mostly) within the realm of learning and development have garnered enterprise interest. The best example is what we now refer to as virtual collaboration. In 2006, before the downturn, webinars (virtual learning) had become popular, but enterprise virtual collaboration had not. If we wanted to buy a platform, IT and procurement helped, but they had no vested interest in the outcome because they did not see themselves as primary, or even big, users.

Today, everyone is all about virtual, and IT departments now lead the acquisition process for these tools, which are an expected part of a company's technical infrastructure. To the novice, the requirements for virtual meetings and virtual learning are the same, so there is no real need to involve learning professionals in the procurement process. It isn't until after we raise questions or request features like breakout rooms, LMS integration, or polls and tests that people realize that all virtual tools are not created equal.

On a related note, IT departments are purchasing technologies with the implicit or explicit expectation that the technologies will be used to deliver training or performance support, without consulting learning professionals about their efficacy. Two examples are social collaboration and, more recently, gamification.

If you asked experienced learning professionals, they would say that both technologies have a role in learning. But like all other cool tools, availability is not, and should not be, the sole consideration for adoption. And early, sometimes anecdotal, evidence suggests that using collaboration tools and gamification in a corporate learning setting is neither as effective nor as popular as one might expect, given their popularity outside work.

This is not to say that social collaboration and gamification have no use in a learning setting. Instead, it is the expectation by others (non-experts) that both should be used as part of learning or performance support solutions that creates that challenge. If those who decide what to purchase use learning and development as a justification to do so, learning professionals will feel pressure to include these tools, even if they add no discernable value to our products. In other words, we risk the loss of control over how we design.

What Hasn't Changed

What isn't different is that thousands of learning professionals are still trying to do the best they can to deliver meaningful development experiences to their clients. And they still have to sift through the unending onslaught of myth, hype, and hyperbole as they try to find efficient and effective solutions to learning problems.

As a result, the goal of this book is no different from the first *Lies About Learning*: To explore the most common lies about learning and then offer some practical tips about how to deal with them. My contributors and I aim to give business executives and learning professionals enough ammunition to ask the right questions, kick the right tires, and maintain the right level of skepticism about what they read and hear about learning products, technologies, and tools. We want to help enable prudent decisions that lead to measurable, predictable, and meaningful results. And we want to tell our story in a way that makes you smile. Figuring all this out is stressful enough. Reading about it ought not to be.

Acknowledgments

I always wonder what inspires people to write. I expect there are as many reasons as writers. Regardless, I am incredibly grateful that the learning industry experts who contributed to this book were sufficiently inspired to advance this effort. I want to thank them for their interest, commitment, perseverance, flexibility, and humility. I appreciate their work more than they know.

I also need to acknowledge my family. Not everyone has the ability to recognize their children in such a public forum, and I greatly appreciate the opportunity. Aron and Ben, your mother and I are incredibly proud of who you are and what you have become. We love you very much. And Wendy, my wife, partner, soul mate, friend, critic, and, perhaps most important, dresser; thank you for giving me the space, both figuratively and literally, to take on projects like this. Because I so enjoy the process of writing and editing, I often forget how much time it actually takes—time I could be spending on other pursuits that you might actually enjoy. Thank you dear; I love you.

Finally, there is my father, Max Israelite, who left us a little more than eight years ago. Among many other gifts, I inherited from him my love of writing. He was prolific, publishing some 900 stories about his life, the lives of his family, his observations on the political and social landscape, and all sorts of other topics that struck a chord with almost everyone who picked up something he had written. I could thank him for many things, but in this context, it is the ability to knock out 800 words at will, something he did every morning for almost 20 years, for which I am most grateful. Thanks, Dad.

Introduction:
Preview of Coming Attractions

Larry Israelite

My wife and I watch a lot of movies. Not by streaming from Netflix or Amazon Prime, but the old-fashioned way—by going to a movie theater. Part of the experience we enjoy is sitting through the previews. The preview, of course, aims to make the viewer really want to see the movie. Wendy and I have a little "thumbs up/thumbs down" system that we invoke at the end of each preview. Sometimes the previews just aren't that interesting (thumbs down). Sometimes we fear that that the producers have crammed so much into the preview that we aren't sure there is anything left to see (thumbs down). But sometimes we are so captivated by the story, the characters, the cinematography, or some other element that we can't wait to see more (two thumbs up). And that, perhaps in a more modest way, is my goal in this introduction.

What I offer you here is a preview of what's to come. I hope to provide enough context to stimulate, tantalize, intrigue, or even outrage you. And I hope to help you identify the chapters that can help you solve an immediate problem or respond to a pressing need, and those that you may want to read at your leisure. In other words, I am trying to provide you with a way to access the content that is, simultaneously, easy and meaningful.

The order of the chapters is not accidental. But it is only fair to mention that it is different from the order I had originally planned. As I read and edited the chapters, a new narrative developed—one based on an approach to entering the world of lies about learning with a particular perspective that I hope you will find useful. That is not to say that one must proceed in the prescribed order. To the contrary, the rules have not changed. The goal is for you to read the chapters from which you will benefit most, just before your personal moment of need.

Part I: Lies About Learning in General

Chapter 1: Lies About Learners

If it weren't for learners we would all have different jobs. They are, after all, our raison d'être. They are one of our key stakeholders—our most ardent supporters and most vocal critics. We seek them out for insight into and feedback on the solutions we create for them and the other stakeholders for whom we work. And, on some occasions, they can be pawns in the larger games of chess that happen in our organizations each and every day. But above all else, they are ever changing and always evolving. And that is precisely the issue that Annmarie Neal and Daniel Sonsino vigorously tackle in their chapter.

Neal and Sonsino propose that the current and, perhaps more important, incoming generation of learners are so fundamentally different from those whom we have served in the past that we have to rethink most of what we know about enabling workplace learning. In fact, we need to rethink almost all of our long-held beliefs and assumptions about talent management in general. While others can, and will, continue to argue about the similarities and differences among Baby Boomers, Gen Xers, and Millennials, Neal and Sonsino focus on the impact that complete and total fluency with technology will have on learning. They explore in great detail the changes that will be required if we are to meet the needs of a workforce that is, in every sense of the phrase, digitally native.

Chapter 2: Lies About Learning Research

In theory, almost everything a learning professional does is based on some sort of scientific research. We do we what we do because professionals with the appropriate expertise conducted studies, evaluated results, and then drew and documented valid conclusions about what they learned. In most cases, the results, conclusions, and recommendations find their way into books, articles, and other documents that, eventually, guide professional practice. We know names like Skinner, Gagné, or Schank, and theories like behaviorism, cognitivism, or construtivism thanks to such research, and they and their theories, both individually and collectively, have forever altered the practice of our collective profession.

In his chapter, Doug Lynch argues that we have become a little sloppy in our approach to research. We have become, it appears, too willing to take on faith that the things we hear at conferences or read in the trade press (notice that I did not use the phrase "refereed journals") are true. We have become less demanding than we should in asking for real evidence that backs up the claims being made. And, even worse, we allow well-publicized, but unproven, hypotheses to take on a mantle of absolute truth and alter the practice of our professions. Lynch offers suggestions for how we can become more critical of the claims we hear and more rigorous in how we determine the difference between truth and desire.

Chapter 3: More Lies About Instructional Design

Most formally trained instructional designers I know spend part of their workday defending the profession. In many cases these defenses aren't overt. Rather, they tend to be more nuanced explanations of what they do, why they do it, what happens if they don't, what difference it makes, and so on. If you are a trained designer, you know the drill—anyone can design. And even worse, each new tool, technology, generation, or almost anything else new and cool may simply eliminate the need for the rigorous application of principles—the art and science—of instructional design.

This isn't new. Looking back on my career, I can identify specific times when pundits, prognosticators, and people with an agenda declared the end of instructional design. New developments in technology, they said, would eliminate the need, assuming there had been one in the first place. History, of course, has proven them wrong over and over again. As it turns out, products intended to enable learning require that people who understand learning, and how it occurs, be involved in creating it. Go figure!

In her chapter, Mindy Jackson tackles this issue head on. In her spirited defense of her profession, she tackles the more recent developments that have given skeptics broader license to argue that instructional design is a quaint relic of an interesting, but largely irrelevant, past.

Part II: Lies About the Business and Management of Learning

Chapter 4: Lies About Managing the Learning Function

As it turns out, Albert Einstein did not say: "Insanity is doing the same thing over and over again and expecting a different result." The phrase first popped up in a slightly different form in, of all places, a Narcotics Anonymous document published in the early 1980s. Less than 20 years later, David van Adelsberg and Edward Trolley published *Running Training Like a Business*, which served as a clarion call to learning professionals everywhere that the days of inwardly focused, output-oriented training organizations were rapidly dwindling. Rather, they contended, training professionals must learn to measure themselves by the outcomes they deliver and, more important, by the value they create for the customers they support. In other words, these professionals had to hold themselves accountable to the same standards as any other business. Unfortunately, 16 years later, it may be that we are all insane, because, in far too many cases, we continue to do the same things we have always done, but we continue to expect different results—more respect, bigger budgets, sufficient resources, and the ever-elusive seat at the table.

In his chapter, Trolley argues that learning leaders can do much more to improve the effectiveness, efficiency, and value of the products and services they deliver to their internal customers. But to do so, they must be willing to stop doing what they have always done and take a fresh look at everything, with an eye toward doing what is best for the organization, even if it means letting go of the functions and resources they have traditionally controlled.

Chapter 5: Lies About Learning to Lead

I have long listened to, participated in, and become sincerely disinterested in the never-ending argument about whether leaders are born, trained, or some combination thereof. And at the same time, there is the ongoing disagreement about whether managers have to be leaders, whether leaders have to be managers, or whether both are, more or less, the same. I suspect that there are several truths and lies about these issues, none of which will be resolved any time soon. It doesn't really matter anyway. And nothing all that useful has ever come from the discussion. That said, I don't expect the discussions to stop any time soon. And, perhaps, we learn something through the process; we refine our personal perspectives or philosophies with what we hear from and say to others.

Leaders—or managers, if you prefer—have their own conversations about their jobs and what it takes to do them well. And just as learning professionals develop points of view about our work, our responsibilities, and the best ways to learn how to fulfill them, leaders do the same. It is precisely this issue that Terry Traut addresses in his chapter—the stories new and experienced leaders tell themselves that prevent them from getting the development they need to increase their capabilities and the likelihood of success. He goes on to describe what learning and development professionals can do to help ensure that leaders take advantage of the available development opportunities.

Chapter 6: Lies About Learning Strategies

Like most people who work in discrete disciplines, learning professionals have a unique vocabulary to describe their work. Some terms we use have commonly accepted—or to outsiders relatively accessible—meanings. Most people will have a shared understanding of what the terms mean and, in many cases, the kind of work or work product they describe. But in other cases, the meaning is not as clear—for example, "learning strategy."

We use that phrase frequently, but do we really know what it means? More important, do our clients—the ones for whom we create these "strategies"—understand what they are, why we create them, and what actual value they deliver? I would guess that most of us would acknowledge that we haven't done a particularly good job of articulating this.

Tina Busch addresses this issue. In her chapter, she suggests that a learning strategy is the component of a larger business strategy that describes how employees will be made capable of delivering what is expected of them. She goes on to describe some of the biggest lies that learning professionals tell themselves, which, in turn, inhibit their ability to effectively develop, communicate, and execute learning strategies that deliver real value to their organizations.

Chapter 7: Lies About the Return on Learning

For some reason, the phrase *return on learning* is one of the third rails of our profession. If we talk about it at all, we do so only in small groups of our most trusted colleagues. We speak in hushed voices, looking over our shoulders to make sure that outsiders aren't listening in, getting ideas, or developing expectations on which we may never be able to deliver. If it weren't such an important issue, we might find this almost comical.

To the cynic, the problem is fairly simple: If we quantify the value of what we deliver, we may find out that we don't deliver nearly as much value as we thought we did, if any at all. And if we are honest, we will acknowledge that it is far easier and much safer to take the position that training has some inherent value—that well-designed, highly interactive programs (classroom or otherwise) have intrinsic value. We say earnestly and often truthfully that our clients lack the ability, interest, or will to collect the information we need to quantify the value and impact of our solutions. So, in many cases, we just don't.

In his chapter, David Vance forcefully argues that we are making a crucial mistake by not aggressively pursuing and implementing a comprehensive strategy for calculating the return on learning. He describes in detail the importance of rigorously measuring the economic value of the products and services we provide, and then systematically lays out the excuses we make—the lies we tell—for not doing so. Finally, he provides recommendations for beginning the return on investment journey.

Part III: Lies About Technology and Learning

Chapter 8: Lies About E-Learning

There is no single topic in our profession about which more has been written and less has been said than e-learning. Starting in the early 1980s, every few years a new method of delivering training through some form of computer technology has captured the headlines—and, unfortunately, the hearts, minds, and pocketbooks of our learning colleagues. Pick your technology, and, beyond any shadow of a doubt, it was expected to replace whatever media you were currently using, allowing you to create learning products more quickly and less expensively, drastically reduce the length of the learning experience, and produce unimaginable increases in learning outcomes. And, of course, things never quite worked out that way.

Why? Because the fundamentals of good learning design don't change, no matter which technologies we bring into the mix. And in our fervor to do well, we sometimes forget this. We look for shortcuts, not from laziness or ill intent, but from our intense desire to respond to the needs of our customers, who want what their customers want: solutions that are good, fast, and cheap—all desirable goals.

Industry pioneer Michael W. Allen tackles the lies about e-learning with his unique perspective of someone who has been there from the beginning, helping shape an entire industry. He carefully describes the e-learning myths that have developed over the years and identifies what to do about them.

Chapter 9: Lies About Learning Technology

Hyperbole is rampant in learning technology. Claims about its future usually sound the same: "This [new technology] will change the face of education forever," or to paraphrase a very well-known learning pundit and columnist: "MOOCs will revolutionize corporate learning and development." Both statements are, of course, exaggerations that have been used for emphasis and effect. And, unfortunately, they have had an effect.

Over the course of my career a similar pattern has emerged. Some new (or reframed) learning technology is released to an unsuspecting public and an alleged new revolution is set to begin—or so say the people who released the technology or those who hope to somehow profit by discussing it or providing consulting for it. To be clear, all involved have a job to do. Product producers need to sell. Pundits need to provide insight, advice, and perspective. And consultants need to make a living. But it may be that we all get carried away with the excitement and develop unfulfillable expectations.

In a very honest and introspective discussion of this issue, Elliott Masie provides a thought-provoking analysis of the factors that contributed to the proliferation of lies about learning technology. More important, he presents a clear and compelling approach for thinking about new learning technologies and concrete methods for identifying how they can deliver real value in our organizations.

Part IV: Wrap-Up

Chapter 10: Lies About Learning Pronouncements

Here is a funny line that appears in almost every quarterly report or financial statement: "Past performance is not necessarily indicative of future results." In fact, these documents often devote an entire section (typically named "Forward-Looking Statements") with lots of legal mumbo jumbo to reiterate, in far too many words, this point. So, more or less, the only part of these documents that we can count on being accurate and truthful is the numbers.

But I get it. One should never assume that a company that has been successful in the past will continue to be so in the future. It does, I suppose, make me a little sad everyone doesn't know this, but that's my problem.

In this chapter, I explore, with the help of an unnamed co-conspirator, some of the pronouncements that we hear or read almost daily, many of which should have been prefaced by the sort of caveats that appear in financial statements: The public should not rely (or act) on anything the company says about what might happen in the future because it could all turn out to be complete and utter fiction. Some of these statements are taken as such absolutes that learning professionals reframe their budgets, change their strategies, or make major investments in technology. In other words, I dissect the statements that have a real impact and try to set the record straight about what they mean and how they should be interpreted.

Chapter 11: Final Words

The final chapter is an attempt to place some context around the lies discussed in the preceding chapters, those that could have been but weren't, and those that we tell ourselves. I would be lying if I said my task was easy, because we do complicated work in a complicated world. As I have said many times before, we all wake up each day and try to fight the good fight, to deliver solutions of substance and value so that our customers can deliver on the expectations that have been created for them.

Earlier I said that the book has been designed to be used as a personal performance support tool. So go ahead and read the chapters in the order that makes the most sense to you. I might suggest you read this one last. But no matter the order, I just hope you find this chapter—and the others before it—useful.

Part I

Lies About Learning
in General

1

Lies About Learners: It's Time to Disrupt the Model of Learning

Annmarie Neal and Daniel Sonsino

Between the birth of the world and 2003, there were five exabytes of information created. We [now] create five exabytes every two days. See why it is so painful to operate in information markets?

—Eric Schmidt, Google CEO, at Google's Atmosphere 2010 conference

Never before has the world been marked by such turbulence, complexity, ambiguity, and relentless speed. An insatiable pursuit of technology is propelling a new era of globalization, economic value creation, innovation, and discovery. The pervasive nature of mobile technology and social networks has increased the size of the network, giving voice and economic opportunity to many who were previously silenced by a lack of connectivity.

For global businesses, these factors necessitate a shift in how, where, by whom, and with whom business is done, how leadership is applied, and how individuals organize to increase productivity while creating new forms of value. This pace of business, technology, and societal change necessitates an accelerated need for innovation and business agility, and, for many, a significant reskilling of the workforce.

Learning professionals can no longer rely on traditional—and soon to be obsolete—career development, talent mobility, and learning practices to drive business impact. Learning and development is thus at a strategic inflection point, if not already in crisis. In this chapter, we hope to provide a wake-up call to those learning professionals whose companies collectively spend billions of dollars a year on learning, leadership development, and training (according to the *2013 State of the Industry* report, ATD estimates that companies invested more than $164 billion in learning and development in 2012)—and to those ecosystem partners providing learning solutions, but not achieving the enduring level of success desired.

Our profession can leap the chasm between traditional talent development practices and those required to support the new workforce—and build the organizational learning systems and cultures to ensure that their investments pay off and drive competitive differentiation and success. Thus, we aim to expose four lies—or assumptions—about learners that we believe must be vigorously challenged to improve our thinking about the future of organizational learning.

It's Time to Challenge Our Assumptions About Learners

If the organizations in which we work must challenge assumptions about their core business models, shouldn't we challenge our assumptions about organizational models, leadership capabilities, and learning practices? If we believe what many are predicting, the future of work over the next decade will look nothing like it does today. In fact, those close to technology disruptions and future work trends predict that nearly 40 percent of the jobs we know today will be disrupted by technology within the next five years. Shouldn't we be vigorously challenging our assumptions about the organizational learner?

As learning professionals, we prepare employees to work in dynamic, fluid businesses that are designed with different organizational structures, where the workplace is defined less by employers and more by ecosystems. We thus set out to challenge four lies about learners:

> Learners want to go somewhere (a university or a corporate learning center) to learn.

> Learners want to learn in order to improve their skills and capabilities.

> Learners want to be taught by experts.

> Learners want to keep learning separate from work.

The Digital Generation

Before we jump into our discussion of the lies about learners, let's step back and set some cultural and psychological context around the key attributes of the worker—and learner—of the future. Or as we call this population, the digital generation.

Tech-savvy. Most of the current workforce has grown up during exponential technology advancement. During the past 10 years alone, the workforce saw disruptive technical innovations including text messaging, file sharing, social networking, search as a new way of life, the entire revolution (and repurposing) of the gaming industry, smartphones, and robots doing work previously done by humans. All will revolutionize the workforce as we know it.

Tech-savvy and multitask masters, the digital generation is constantly exchanging messages, surfing the web, and openly participating in social networks using their mobile and gaming devices. They know how to navigate hundreds, if not thousands, of Internet sites and mobile apps that enable them to develop their own content, engage in social learning communities, and even plan their lives and careers.

Collaborative and connected. With access to social, open-source, and mobile technologies, this digital generation is collaborative in work and life and always connected. And as a generation, they were raised to be active team members in academic (learning teams) and recreational (organized sports) activities. So it should be no surprise that as workers, they harness the collaborative intelligence of personal and professional networks and ecosystems—whether in their organization or in their broader network and community.

Flexibility in how they work, live, learn, and play. Developing careers rapidly, learning in the moment, and taking on new experiences are the realities of the new workforce. For the digital generation, work isn't a place you go, but, rather, it is what you do to contribute to the organization, and society more broadly. Work is not just about earning income. This generation of worker places much more emphasis on personal and social enrichment and fulfillment, meaning that they not only need flexibility in how, when, and where work and learning take place, but they also need to see the relevance of what they are doing or learning and its broader application.

"I can do anything" mentality. Confident, raised with a parenting style that built self-esteem at an early age, and not afraid to fail, the digital generation expects to succeed. With this confidence comes an insatiable search-and-explore nature regarding how, when, and where they want and need to work and learn. Our learning systems need to support this exploratory mentality, ensure that developmental opportunities are easy to find, and work with managers to reset assumptions about how to support their expectations.

Lies About Learners

Our current learning approach is outdated. Now is the time to reinvent it. The global business environment is changing rapidly; access to sophisticated, social, digital technologies is increasing; and the digital generation's expectations of how, when, where, and why work gets done are shifting. The learner needs to be at the center of our reinvention. In this section, we aim to create a dialogue that moves us beyond developing learning programs to developing learner-centric learning ecosystems that allow our learners to not only master content—but to thrive with it.

Lie #1: Learners Want to Go Somewhere to Learn

Learning at any time, any place, any path, any pace!
—*Milton Chen, Edutopia*

The first lie—or assumption—is that learners need a break from their hectic work setting, and thus need a peaceful and tranquil environment to soak in and apply content. Instructor-led delivery of training content continues to lead the way when it comes to formal programs, but most learners prefer an anytime, any place, any path, and any pace approach to learning.

If we believe the classroom is where people learn best—and this is validated by industry studies—how does this mesh with changing workplace demographics? In 2012, IDC stated that 1.3 billion people would work remotely using mobile technology by 2015—that's nearly 40 percent of the workforce. To continue with traditional classroom learning settings while the workforce becomes increasingly mobile would be to ignore the needs of our audience, preferring to stick with the methods with which we feel most comfortable.

In the mid-1990s, many within the learning and development profession thought e-learning was the answer. And for many, this approach has allowed for scaling learning through online technology. But it has proved less than adequate in developing critical thinking and innovation skills and, even worse, in developing problem-solving approaches. During the past 10 years, the shift has been toward blended programs, combining classroom and e-learning content. But again, this approach seems to miss the mark with current- and future-based workforce and workplace trends.

Gaming, cyber simulations, and mobile and social tools are all trying to fill the void, but for many organizations these approaches are expensive and time-consuming to conceptualize and develop. However, they represent social engagement and learning trends that we just cannot ignore.

With learners that are increasingly mobile, learning professionals need to meet them where they want to learn, not where we want to teach them. So we must address three critical factors if we are to bring learning methods up to date with the needs of learners:

> **Align learning content with the pace of business.** Does learning content keep pace with the speed of the business? How long does it take to design and launch a learning program? Does that mesh with your company's product development timeframe?

> **Engage learners emotionally, intellectually, and socially with anytime, anywhere learning.** How can a high-engagement, (cyber) simulation-like experience merge with the increasing pace of technological advancements (cloud, apps on devices) so that training professionals can deliver creative, engaging, and immersive experiences?

> **Create real-time immersive experiences.** As technology continues to permeate our daily lives, how do we create social learning environments that leverage these technologies (mobile, sensors, augmented reality) to enable our learners to learn about and interact with the world in a highly engaging, immersive way?

To us, the answers are in how we accelerate the blended approach, combining all the tools in our learning portfolio while adding several new social learning tools to meet the needs of our digital-minded workforce.

Imagine a scenario in which we are location agnostic. Learning is available on demand—it can be consumed whenever, wherever, and however. In this new world, we bring the learning to users and no longer expect them to sit in a traditional classroom, subject to the trainer's availability. To achieve this ambitious goal, we must assess our approaches to learning to identify ways that we can blend mobile, social, mentoring, and both synchronous and asynchronous approaches to create immersive experiences that fully (and frequently) engage learners anytime, anywhere, and on their terms.

Lie #2: Learners Want to Learn in Order to Improve Their Skills and Capabilities

The second lie is that the more skills learners put on their resumes, the faster they expect to be given new opportunities or be promoted. But according to a 2012 Deloitte study, the skills graduates acquire after four years of college have an expected shelf life of only five years, meaning that skills learned in school may become outdated long before student loans are paid off. To meet the needs of our learners and our employers, we must shift our mindset from developing skills to developing learning agility.

Learning professionals often embark on program design with one end in mind: to improve relevant skills in the workplace. We measure return on investment to prove to business leaders that their investments in development are both valuable and relevant. We question this traditional approach because as soon as we train or certify someone in one skill, there are 100 more skills that must follow. And that only includes the skills we are aware of; there are probably many others. If we continue to play the skill game, we will undoubtedly lose.

Traditionally, learning and development professionals have been told to create environments that enable learners to learn. We challenge this premise, and strongly suggest that we shift our focus to developing learning agility, which stems from the ability to engage in rich personal growth and complex problem solving. If we can establish a culture of personal growth and problem solving, we can outpace the skills race.

Think back to high school algebra—back when we had to memorize equations. We now realize that if we had learned to understand the theory and to apply the theory to multiple situations through the use of problem solving, we would have been far better equipped to solve current and future issues. And there would have been no need to memorize specific equations.

The skills gap becomes more apparent the higher you go in the organization. At senior levels, decision making, prioritization, influence, and problem-solving skills have become prerequisites for success; specific technical skills have become less relevant. This may be why executive development programs have started to focus on building the strengths necessary for the future, rather than skills that may become outdated once the program is over.

Imagine a world in which our primary focus is learning to learn—a world in which exercising the mind is as important as exercising the body. For learning professionals, this is a major shift in thinking. It also represents a major shift in how we must justify investments in learning and development to our stakeholders and partners. Successful professionals will embrace this new challenge, move away from their traditional focus on competencies and skills, and rapidly shift their emphasis to higher-level functional development.

Lie #3: Learners Want to Be Taught by Experts

Organizations need to shift in thinking—from fixing what's wrong to unleashing what is possible.

—Angel Mendez, SVP and Chief Transformation Officer, Cisco Systems

The third lie is that learners want to be taught by thought leaders, university professors, consultants, and professional trainers. Many learning professionals continue to believe that the transfer of knowledge is critical to the success of their learning programs. But we are coming to understand that the digital generation would rather turn to their social networks and global online communities to learn what they need, rather than engage in formal, instructor-led learning.

Learning methods have not changed for decades; how we design learning experiences was developed by the military more than 60 years ago to rapidly train soldiers for World War II. Most of our learners still sit in classrooms (physical or online) while an instructor transmits content. While the instructor-led learning model worked in the industrial age, it breaks down in an information economy.

While instructors are considered the experts, many are only concretely knowledgeable about the subjects they are teaching. Instructors tend to stick to the subjects with which they are most comfortable and pass on their own, often narrow, views. Curious learners thus lose the opportunity to look at problems from different perspectives, a capability essential to success in today's business context.

If we think about it, the instructor at the head of the class is not unlike the now outdated hierarchical business model, with a leader at the top whose primary responsibility was keeping things under control and moving efficiently through the tasks at hand. Just as corporate hierarchies are under pressure to change, so too are top-down learning environments that no longer work in today's fast-changing and collaborative business environment.

So, how are our learners learning? Are our learning and development organizations unleashing what's possible, as Angel Mendez suggests? To unleash the possible, we need to move away from an expert model of instruction (aligned to specific content domains) and build on social community structures for learning and sharing. Imagine a learning environment in which employees learn in diverse social communities—communities focused, for example, on a particular engineering problem that they are trying to solve, a product innovation they are trying to launch, or even a business model they need to transform.

Learners no longer have to rely solely on formal learning programs to acquire knowledge. The Internet, after all, can fill that role. But they do need to be encouraged to develop social networks and create learning communities in order to master broader discovery skills, question legacy, observe new ways of thinking and problem solving, and experiment in collaboration with others.

Imagine an organization where learning (not training) is the highest priority and where learning communities prosper. Imagine if employee development was organized around what's most relevant to their day-to-day activities, interests, and passions. And imagine if learning was powered by social networks and technology, rather than by instructors and classrooms. This is how a learning culture will thrive.

According to the Corporate Leadership Council, only 23 percent of business leaders reported satisfaction with the overall effectiveness of their learning function. If these data were reflective of a sales or supply chain organization, those who lead these functions would, surely, be exited from the organization. As learning professionals and experts, we need to put our profession under greater scrutiny. Completely changing our model from learning programs to self-guided social discovery should not seem like career suicide. Why? Because the Corporate Leadership Council also tells us that experiential learning improves engagement by 260 percent and boosts employee performance by 300 percent. We need to listen and lead.

Lie #4: Learners Want to Keep Learning Separate From Work

The fourth—and final—lie we'll cover here is that when employees want to learn, they want to stop what they are doing and attend a scheduled class, book an hour to complete e-learning content, or search the web for relevant content or a job aid. But when employees stop their work processes to learning something new, productivity comes to a halt. Future employee learning will occur as a result of highly personalized, intelligent knowledge management systems that bring content specific to the task at hand to the learner, just in time.

To avoid intruding into business processes, learning professionals have to redesign their approaches to integrate, not interfere, with an employee's workflow. This requires bringing learning to employees and integrating it into functional tools that are used within an organization. Embedded learning objects, social experts, chat functions, and central repositories of critical knowledge—all are examples of learning that must be fully integrated into the processes in which employees work.

In addition to embedding learning within the workflow, companies can support employees beyond the traditional day-to-day work cycle. For example, gamers can use the same online, collaborative approaches to learn work-related, problem-solving skills. Marketing professionals can apply the creative approaches in their personal and social collaboration lives to their work by engaging with their current and future customers in the same ways that they engage with their families and friends. Learning must come from within and across the organization's ecosystem of customers, employees, and partners, drawing from professional networks, social communities, and the passion each individual brings to the organization. The key for learning professionals is to find creative approaches to nurture this learning within the organization.

Imagine a scenario in which an employee is challenged by a work task—such as selling a new product to a customer—but can learn how to solve the challenge the moment it arises. Imagine if this sales employee could simply ask the company's internal virtual assistant, knowledge system, or network of content mentors for help. And imagine that the response was practically instantaneous. The employee wouldn't have to search the LMS for relevant content and then wait for an available classroom program, plod through a badly designed or only partly relevant e-learning program, or navigate the company's intranet for information that may or may not be useful. Instead, the employee could learn immediately within his current business processes or workflow.

It's Time to Disrupt the Model

To get in front of and fully support this changing environment—to disrupt the traditional model—we offer some examples of ways you can challenge yourself daily.

The growing trend among businesses is toward more open and collaborative networks. How can we disrupt the learning and development platform to create an innovative learning experience—maybe even something that approaches an open-source model—that still creates value for all learners? How can we reward learners for both the quality of their ideas and their ability (and willingness) to co-create and share knowledge? Some growing movements toward open-access and open-knowledge models are the TED Talks and the Kahn Academy. These movements will only grow stronger, as a generation that has grown up sharing everything—and expecting everything to be shared—assumes a more influential role in business and society.

We need a new business model around knowledge itself. A business model based on developing and selling knowledge (training) no longer works in an age when content is increasingly free and accessible. Knowledge should no longer be treated as a standalone product. The marketplace values the ability to share that knowledge so that others can apply it, enhance it, and create even greater value from it. How does this translate to those in the business of learning and development?

As the technology choices and options become simpler, the learning executive becomes less of a trainer and more of a community curator—creating social networks and learning communities that help learners figure out how to solve business problems, rather than telling them what training courses to take. We need to challenge learning system providers to consider these trends and meet our needs. All too often we take the available systems as they are, sealing our own fate by launching outdated tools.

We need to challenge the performance systems used by so many companies that serve as barriers to taking a broader organizational approach to learning. These industrial-age systems encourage competition among individuals, rather than fostering experimentation, risk taking, and collaboration. All this despite the fact that elite performance and engagement comes from meaningful work with fully engaged colleagues who collaborate to solve complex problems for a company, an industry, and society at large. We cannot establish a culture of learning if we rely on systems that devalue that culture. It's that simple.

Conclusion

Our complex, globalized, and highly technological business environments demand new business models, new management models, and new ways of creating systems for organizational learning. As our organizations evolve to support an innovation economy, so too must our understanding of how employees engage with content to remain productive in the future—how learners learn.

New social learning platforms and technologies are forcing an unprecedented reorganization of how we develop, curate, and deliver learning content at scale. Having a social networking (or social learning) presence is no longer optional. Employees expect it in order to connect to their co-workers, their ecosystem partners, and their communities of practice. In many industries, employees are expected to engage in vital conversations, build trusted relationships, and learn. So traditional forms of learning are yielding to entirely new development programs that are social, mobile, continuous, and highly integrated with broader business strategies.

Our learning tools must not just serve to retain and train the workforce. They will need to shape the socially structured organizations that we will inhabit in an information economy and where innovation is essential to sustained market differentiation. Immersive learning strategies—such as sophisticated workplace games—are engaging learners to solve problems and co-create solutions, while open education platforms are increasingly making content available just in time to everyone that wants, or needs, to learn.

The future is fraught with risk, change, investment, and personal and professional sacrifice—but also with incredible promise. Are you ready, willing, and able to take the steps to accelerate your organization's success? Now is the time for you to decide.

References

The American Society for Training & Development (ASTD). 2013. *2013 State of the Industry.* Alexandria, VA: ASTD Press.

Eggers, W.D., and J. Hagel. 2012. *Brawn From Brains: Talent, Policy, and the Future of American Competitiveness.* Deloitte University Press, September 27. http://dupress.com/articles/brawn-from-brains-talent-policy-and-the-future-of-american-competitiveness.

2

Lies About Learning Research

Doug Lynch

The learning profession has a propensity for promoting inaccuracy and lies. In the simplest terms, a lie is a falsehood, and in that sense, anything that ends up being ultimately untrue could be interpreted as a lie. But in the messy world of social science and corporate learning, such a standard isn't practical. A more precise definition of a lie implies an intent to deceive. Sadly, because of its messiness and our own lack of conviction in the efficacy of what we do, our space is fraught with well-intentioned lies.

My focus in this chapter is on the lies designed to gloss over the messiness of our world with respect to research on the effectiveness of what we do. At its core, research is simply a systematic investigation. This concept is important to practitioners because there is a false dichotomy common in our world, which, if accepted, becomes a lie—that research and practice are somehow at odds. A related lie is that tension also exists between theory and practice. These two lies—that theory and research are at odds with practice—become clear if you tease at them. Everything you do is grounded in a theory and when you do what you do, you are conducting research. You simply can't get around it.

Here is an example. There are three theories that explain gravity: quantum mechanics, Einsteinian, and Newtonian. None of these theories is a truth. Each is backed by research—that is, a systematic investigation that led to some empirical evidence that supports the theory; each also has research that refutes it. Turns out quantum mechanics does a great job of explaining how gravity interacts among very small things like particles, but a poor job of explaining how gravity interacts with very large objects like galaxies. Einstein's work does the opposite. Newton did a great job explaining how gravity works for the likes of you and me (the apple falling from the tree), but Newtonian physics falls apart if you are trying to map the universe or work with particles. All three theories are very practical, and we use them—or products based on them—every day. The key for practitioners, in this case engineers, is to know which theory to apply to frame the questions they wish to explore or the problems they wish to solve. We are, in essence, learning engineers and, as engineers, we need to know the guiding theories.

Not being fluent in theory and research sets us up to either accept lies or perpetuate lies, and that affects how we interpret our systematic investigation of our work as learning professionals. Each of us conducts and consumes research daily. As a result, our consumption and production of research can impede our success. We need to be informed consumers and producers of research on corporate learning. We need to know when vendors are deceiving us. And we need to be careful when we make proclamations about our own success. Why? Because in a knowledge economy, how we develop people is important to our companies, employees, and society.

There is ample research suggesting that learning is a beneficial endeavor, and when done right, it helps not only the company, but also employees and the broader economy. This chapter will encourage you to be thoughtful when you make claims about what you do and to be careful when you are evaluating what others say they can do. I will present some examples that illustrate my statement as a reasonable hypothesis and present some evidence for you to evaluate. I will end the chapter with some practical tips you can follow as a learning professional and with a call to arms for us as a community. But let me start by urging you to not take anything I state prima facie. Investigate it more thoroughly yourself.

Research, Theory, and You

My claim is that you are already a researcher and, perhaps even more uncomfortably, you are a learning theorist. How so? Well, as a learning professional you engineer change and you need theory and research to execute that change. The questions before us in the field are how aware are we that we do these two things and how good are we at theorizing and researching corporate learning. Let's look at the theories that underpin why we do what we do.

But first, let's deal with the content—the "what" of the work you do. Let's acknowledge that all the content you deliver is somehow empirically vetted. Whether it is emotional intelligence or strategy, you got the content somewhere and someone posited a theory to explain a behavior and researched it. I worry about the veracity of much of the popular trends that business executives consume, but for our purposes let's put that aside and focus on the how and why of what we do when we provide learning and development solutions to help our employees grow and companies succeed.

As you identify a business problem and develop the corresponding intervention, you operate at the intersection of two theoretical concepts grounded in the economic literature. The first is human capital theory, which suggests that you can make people more productive if you invest in them through development. Everything you do is predicated on this one theory that has ample evidence supporting it. At the same time, however, some evidence suggests that a second, competing theory (signaling) may also be obfuscating the impact of your development in increasing human capital.

Given that this competing theory also has ample evidence and can get in the way of the efficacy of your development efforts, it is worth taking a moment to discuss it. Signaling basically says that when you decide to develop someone you are simply sending a signal to the market—managers, co-workers, and so on—that this person is different, rather than actually making her more productive. Economists have found evidence supporting this competing theory. For example, two separate studies, one by Thomas J. Kane at Harvard and the other by Alan B. Krueger at Princeton, investigated the value of an Ivy League degree. They both found ample evidence that the market pays a premium for such a pedigree, but when they investigated further and controlled for "endowments" (think of these as individual traits such as intelligence and work ethic), they found that the evidence suggested it was more of a signal than the result of any additional learning taking place at these schools.

These ways of thinking about people development are based on the ideas of James Heckman, a Nobel Laureate who won the medal for work in this area. And it appears that other economists think there is merit to these approaches. While it may seem contradictory that these two theories compete, keep in mind that James Joyce said the sign of true genius is keeping competing ideas in your head simultaneously.

Let me give you a concrete example with which you may be familiar—high-potential programs. Being selected by a company to be part of a high-potential program may do two things, which compete with each other from a design perspective. It may be that these programs actually increase the capabilities of those who attend. But simply being selected to participate also sends a signal—to the company, other employees, and the participants themselves—about their talent separate from what they gain in the program. If all we are doing is sending a signal, making it a rite of passage into upper management, we might design the program very differently than if the only reason we are doing it is to develop some future leader who has some latent potential.

Even though these two theories compete, they both suggest why development may be a viable, and perhaps differentiating, business strategy.

Now we turn to how you implement development, and recognize that it, too, is governed by theories backed by research. With learning theories, there are also competing theories, and it is important to own your assumptions because they influence your design and evaluation. There are three competing theories of learning, each (like the physics example) with significant empirical evidence to support them: behaviorist, cognitivist, and sociocultural. You should be fluent in these theories in the same way engineers are fluent in physics and the competing theories of gravity.

Every time you design or deliver a program, you are making theoretical assumptions; they are embedded in how you build your program. And if you are evaluating learning, even if it is simply with a smile sheet, you are conducting research. But if you are not clear and explicit, chances are you're not maximizing the impact of what you do. And that lack of clarity will lead to perpetuating lies about learning.

Setting the Bar for Truth in Our World

Now that we are aware that we are all theorists and researchers, let's talk about the paradigms that we use to empirically evaluate our evidence. The reason to focus our energies here is that it is the crux of how we decide whether to continue doing what we do or to try something different. If something works, we are likely to continue to do it; if it doesn't, we are likely to try something different. There are two popular approaches to evaluating what works. Neither approach has significant traction among top researchers as a particularly compelling empirical approach, but they do among corporate learning professionals.

The most common approach to evaluating the efficacy of what we do is the Kirkpatrick model. Conceptually, this model is quite elegant; it gives us a framework and model that we all grasp. It might be more useful if we didn't think of the levels as ordinal (four is better than one) but rather as categorical (four is different from one). However, the problem that I have seen, at least anecdotally, is how the model is applied empirically. Because we tend to see the conceptual model as ordinal, we aspire to reach the top level. Consequently, we tend to pay less attention to how we measure at the desired level and how we analyze the data because, as Robert Browning said, "a man's reach must exceed his grasp" (Browning 1933). Consequently, we often don't measure and analyze accurately, and yet those two concepts are at the heart of effective research or a systematic investigation.

For example, a Level 4 case study is not the way a financial analyst would gather empirical evidence to measure efficacy.

I'll spend more time on this later in the chapter. But here's another example to illustrate my point. Scientists are curious about measuring the age of our world and have different ways of gathering evidence to explore this. One way would be to use annual Gallup data from surveys asking what most Americans believe. However, if one were to use that evidence and then regress it, one might find that the age of the earth is approximately 6,000 years. While such an approach is statistically valid and reliable, in some cases it might not be the best way of answering the question. Surveying Americans is an effective way of determining what they believe, but even though it is measured accurately and analyzed correctly, the underlying data are fraught with error. A better approach might be to use radiometric dating; such an approach might produce less reliable results in terms of the margin of error (when estimating the age of rocks there is variance of several million years), but, ultimately, a more accurate answer to the question.

The other common approach to evaluating learning is Brinkerhoff's Success Case Method, which is about telling success stories. Conceptually, one is not looking for typical outcomes, but, rather, extraordinary outcomes. So if you can find one instance where something amazing happened, that is the story to tell in this methodology. The logic of this approach is that performance is described based on the extremes rather than a mean or median score.

Indeed, the paleontologist Stephen Jay Gould wrote of his own mortality in this vein in "The Median Isn't the Message" when he learned that the average life expectancy for someone with his form of cancer was less than a year and yet he lived many years after developing the cancer (Gould 1985). The median or mean is simply part of a description of a distribution. At the same time, outliers are also parts of the distribution and much less likely to occur than a mean or median.

So the Brinkerhoff approach is akin to telling the story of someone who survived falling out of a plane at 36,000 feet and then using that information to justify jumping out of a plane without a parachute. I certainly find this approach compelling in terms of advocacy; reading about someone who survives a plane crash or beats the odds of cancer is motivating. But such an approach is less compelling in terms of research because it suggests that an atypical outcome is typical. Following this logic, from an analytical perspective, it also suffers from the shortcomings of some implementations of the Kirkpatrick model: case studies, which might be wonderful for contextualizing what happened, are generally not accepted by scientists for explaining causal relationships.

Some Current Whoppers in the World of Corporate Research

Let's first recognize that vendors, when advertising or providing testimonials on the efficacy of some software or training, are explicitly trying to mislead you. This doesn't mean that they are not providing value, but they are not motivated to conduct systematic investigations on the limitations of their products. More troubling to me are the examples of pervasive misinformation that I've seen in our profession. I understand the motivation, because there is a perception and some plausible evidence that the public and companies undervalue learning. But when we behave that way, we may undermine our own credibility because we generate and perpetuate what can be broadly construed as lies.

Three of the most popular business books of all time are fraught with deceptions of various sorts, yet we continue to buy them and believe them. Perhaps the most upsetting is *In Search of Excellence* (Peters and Waterman 1982), where one of the authors admitted that some data were faked (Byrne 2001). Another great book, *The Seven Habits of Highly Effective People* is largely aspirational and based on Stephen R. Covey's strong religious grounding and ethics (Covey 1989). He argues that if people behaved more in this way, companies would be better off. But there wasn't any thorough empirical testing of the hypothesis. So while I think his book is great, and inspirational in its aspirations, it has been interpreted as something that it is not. In the literature, I could find no evidence of whether adopting the habits advocated in the book is an effective leadership strategy.

The third book is Jim Collins's (2001) *Good to Great*, which is simply guilty of poor research design. Collins got his evidence by looking for patterns in behavioral traits among leaders of successful companies. But then he argues that these patterns are generalizable. In other words, any leader that adopted these traits would make his company great. The best way to investigate the question, once the traits had been identified, would have been to identify two groups of leaders who were similar, except for having those traits, randomly distributing them as CEOs at companies, and then evaluating company performance. Clearly, this is impractical, but he could have at least run a broader sample to see if there was any evidence of the same behaviors existing in companies that weren't so great. One could have also easily investigated whether endogeneity was present (this is kind of a methodological chicken-and-egg question—do great companies make great leaders or vice versa).

This attention to detail in how a question is asked may seem trite, but I can give you two examples that illustrate its importance. You could run a pattern of the traits of the best basketball teams and then generalize that you only need tall African Americans to put together a great team. Or you could find that drug use is quite prevalent among musicians and that all you need to do to be a rock star is consume illicit drugs. We need to be fluent consumers of business research and pay particular attention to how the hypotheses put forth are systematically investigated. If we don't hold authors to some minimum standard of investigatory rigor, we are guilty of perpetuating the falsehoods.

Now let's move on to examples grounded purely in our world, where we are the producers of the theory and the research, rather than consumers of it. Let's start with an example that represents a commonly perpetuated lie—the notion of learning styles. Generally, a learning style refers to the way an individual acquires and processes content. The hypothesis is that different people learn differently and that if one does not align an individual's learning style with the delivery of content, then learning will not occur. What is so interesting about this example is that it is so pervasive and popular, even though it has been thoroughly researched and there is overwhelming evidence against it. Indeed, there have been more than 100 peer-reviewed studies investigating this hypothesis, and they all found no evidence of differences in how people learn. Even when people self-identified with a particular learning style and then had content delivered consistent with that style, there was no increase in learning. In other words, there is overwhelming evidence that people learn in many different ways but no evidence that designing to accommodate an individual's style preference leads to better outcomes. Despite the overwhelming evidence, if you search for "corporate learning" and "learning styles" you get close to 4.5 million hits.

So why do I still hear companies talking about building or buying programs to accommodate a particular learner's style? The primary reason, I suspect, is that the myth (that learning styles matter) simply sounds better than the truth (that they don't). Both buyers and consumers of content feel better when they believe that their unique needs have been considered when a product was designed. And arguing that learning styles are not nearly as relevant as we think earns us no credibility and, in fact, may even hurt us because, for better or worse, the myth has been accepted as truth in the marketplace of learning ideas. So we just choose to let it slide, recognizing that we are perpetuating what is, for all intents and purposes, a lie.

Another lie involves making an inaccurate inference from observational data. Think of this as a rendition of an old show tune from *Bye Bye Birdie*—"what's the matter with kids today?" The prevailing argument uses the following logic: A manager notices that the younger people in the office work differently than the older people and then assumes that there is something fundamentally different about younger workers today (the popular pieces started appearing when Generation X was entering the workforce and now it is applied to Millennials). This presumption is a classic example of misinterpreting a generational effect for a cohort effect. Peter Cappelli, the George W. Taylor professor of management and director of the Center for Human Resources at the Wharton School of Business, has written about this eloquently. There is no evidence that humans have evolved into some new species since the birth of Millennials. And as the old musical song attests, folks have been observing that young people seem different from older people since time immemorial. This is what research circles call a specification error.

Next, let me give an example that is akin to embellishment. It is a good theory but one that has never been researched effectively (and, by definition, probably never will)—most learning happens informally. When I search for this "informal learning" on the web, I get more than 14 million hits. Note that I am not arguing that informal learning does not exist. Many peer-reviewed articles have investigated it, most recently a Stanford study used by the White House for public policy purposes. But what has not been vetted is this ratio of 70-20-10, despite a host of articles written about it.

From what I was able to ascertain when attempting to follow the literature, this was akin to that old childhood game of telephone. In the 1960s a Canadian researcher, Allen Tough, posited that one could think of the relationship between informal learning and formal learning like an iceberg. It seems that over time, someone, or perhaps many people, took that metaphor, attached weights to it, and all of a sudden it became an accepted notion that 90 percent of learning is informal and people budgeted accordingly. But how does one even measure that? It is now accepted as a truth, and meaningful decisions are made based on it. We should infer from this that, while informal learning exists, by definition we cannot structure it or measure it, and we certainly should not assign ratios to it and budget accordingly.

My final example relates to return on investment (ROI)—the holy grail among corporate learners. I first heard this term applied to the world of corporate learning when a chief learning officer (CLO) from a Fortune 100 company publically proclaimed an ROI of 1,328 percent. I was shocked at such a statement. There is a rich history in the literature of labor economics on estimating the returns on education. Calculating ROI is one way to measure return on education; net present value or optionality approaches are also options. To put the 1,328 percent in context, economists using various econometric models have estimated that most returns on a high-quality college education hover between 10 and 20 percent. So if this company had really cracked this nut, then it meant it was performing 100 times as well as, say, Harvard Business School. One need only look at the balance sheet and income statement to realize that what was happening instead was very poor research.

Now to be clear, there is ample evidence on the returns on education and it has been quantified, so it can be calculated. And I understand the compelling arguments around the need for learning leaders to have more business acumen and talk the language of business. But if you went to the chief financial officer (CFO) with such a claim, it would not be laudable, but laughable. CFOs understand conceptually the notion of return on education, and they also probably know that those returns are not best measured as ROI.

Think about it. ROI implies that one can look at a company's financial performance over time, take into account all the extraneous variables that would affect that company, quantify all the costs associated with delivering the program, isolate the endowment effects (such as motivation, prior education, and intelligence), and come up with a simple ratio. In theory, one could use stock price, because it is supposed to take into account both the market effects and future earnings, but even so it is a fool's errand. This is a classic example of poor research design. It is a plausible question supported by theory, although not sufficiently practical to execute for the average CLO. Trying to measure returns on corporate learning using ROI is like trying to turn lead into gold.

What These Things Have in Common

What lessons can we draw from these examples? Well, I hope you see that we are all in good company when making these mistakes. Being diligent is difficult when you are under financial and time pressure. Perhaps trickier is that, as professionals, we have our own experiences to draw from, and those experiences shape our views of the world. But because we may know from experience that something is there and we are under pressure to perform, we too often act more like learning advocates, as opposed to learning engineers. What matters to our employers and to us is that we help the business, not that we have a large budget or lots of programs. We should put our heart and soul into the design and delivery of programs. But at the end of the day, the programs need to stand or fall on their merits, and we should always have the best interests of the organization and our colleagues in the forefront, rather than the creativity or coolness of our programs.

We need to stop being lemmings. We are so enamored with the next great trend that we jump on these bandwagons, partially because the success of our programs matters so much. But we need to be much more thoughtful in how we interpret the research we are consuming to inform our program designs. And we need to recognize that the way we ask a question matters most because we cannot fix through clever analysis that which we messed up in design.

How to Prevent Getting Hoodwinked and Lying to Yourself

The key to ensuring that you aren't deceived or don't inadvertently deceive is to be an effective theoretician and researcher. What does that mean? First, pose questions (and by definition answers) that can be tested—investigated empirically. Better to measure what you can measure well—say, a Level 2 Kirkpatrick evaluation—than aspire to do a Level 4 evaluation and use self-reported data to say that you've measured business impact.

Second, know your underlying theory and link your questions to it. Imagine using a behavioral approach for compliance training, a cognitive approach for strategy, and perhaps a social theory approach for innovation. You should know which pedagogical approach you are using and why.

Whenever possible, use methods that permit direct investigation of your questions. If you want to see if someone can do something, don't ask if she can do it, ask her to demonstrate that she can do it. If you want to know if he found the course useful, ask him whether he found it useful. Be clear and thoughtful about how you measure things and do it as directly as possible.

Third, provide a coherent and explicit chain of reasoning; walk yourself through how you got to the question. For example, before you run a sales training program, make sure you understand why you're running the program. What evidence do you have that it is a skills problem (as opposed to a slow economy)? What evidence do you have that it is a performance problem that cuts across individuals, as opposed to some other thing that may be influencing sales, such as the product itself or sales support? Then investigate why you are running a particular intervention. How do you know that is the right choice compared with a different program that might be available in the marketplace? Make sure you have a strategy in place for evaluating success before running the program. Perhaps one approach would be to run the intervention once as an experiment to test the hypothesis and then repeat, evaluating all the way. You could also see if others have investigated the question before you and learn from their results. Finally, whenever possible, disclose research to encourage professional scrutiny and debate. This makes all of us better.

Let's review two research approaches: collecting numbers (quantitative) and collecting observations (qualitative). Keep in mind that all social sciences ask the same basic sorts of questions, so all the approaches are relevant. But each approach is like a lens, and it brings certain things into focus and moves other things out of focus.

We probably should be conducting research that is a mix of qualitative and quantitative, with a heavy emphasis on quantitative methods. When it comes to developing people, it is important to recognize that you aren't ever going to be able to capture the full impact of any training; learning is too complex, there are so many interaction effects, and learning doesn't happen the way it was conceived in the popular *Matrix* movies series, where you only need to plug in and download knowledge. Performance and learning are loosely coupled; some takes time to stick and some lasts quite a long time. Thus, there are always some consumption and investment benefits to training, and there are individual and social benefits to learning. So you might not be able to take a course on innovation and turn a company around overnight, but the course might spark a bulb that generates a solution in the future. Or you might take a course that benefits your team as much as yourself.

Going beyond these conceptual ideas, how we systematically gather evidence means different things and answers questions differently. For empirical investigations, we could conduct interviews, run statistical analyses of data—either observational or self-reported—or we could conduct controlled experiments. Even with the same data and the same paradigm, we can analyze things differently with different measurement techniques. We could use simple correlation, a residual approach that controls for other factors, or we could measure direct returns. The example I gave earlier about investigating the age of the earth gets at this idea, even though both the survey and direct investigation of the rocks were analyzed quantitatively. Remember, the most direct approach is generally the better approach.

Finally, if we are interested in things like the value of training, we need to be aware of measurement challenges, such as the interaction of education, prior education, and ability; selectivity bias; the quality versus the quantity of training; and discounting for time. Two strategy courses, one taught by Bob the Builder and the other by Michael Porter, shouldn't be treated the same. And a great course that provides benefits to the company 10 years down the road needs to be evaluated differently from the great course that provides benefits tomorrow.

The Hierarchy of Evidence for Impact

Generally, the more times something has been tested, the better. So you would rather use a tool, product, or intervention that 100 studies say works, rather than simply rely on one study with the same finding (with the huge caveat that the quality of each study matters).

If you are attempting to demonstrate impact, the gold standard among researchers is randomized control trials; they are the classic experiments that scientists use with control groups. Almost as good are natural experiments and quasi-experiments. Less desirable are the survey and case study, which happen to be the ones that we see most often in our space. While the survey and case study tell us things, they don't answer the question of whether something worked or not. Surveys can tell us what people say and, if well designed, what people think, but they are less accurate at telling us what people do. Case studies are spectacular at illustrating a point, but suffer from the same problems that surveys suffer from, plus the added constraint of generally having a sample size of one. As a result, it is difficult to make inferences with respect to generalizability.

Why Research Matters

In some fundamental ways, all social scientists are interested in answering the same sorts of questions about the world. But each discipline has very specific rules about the fidelity of research and is concerned about poorly designed and executed mixed-method research. With respect to education evaluation, the U.S. Government's Office of Management and Budgets, the Campbell Collaborative, and National Academy of Sciences have attempted to describe a hierarchy of evidence where, roughly speaking, there is consensus:

➤ More studies are better than fewer.

➤ Anecdotal case studies or testimonials are the weakest form of evidence.

➤ Randomized controlled experiments are the gold standard.

And there is recognition that some approaches are better at revealing hypotheses and exploring why others are better at evaluating whether something worked as planned. Table 2-1 lists some purposes or goals of research and the corresponding approaches.

Table 2-1. Research Methods and Their Goals

Research Methods	Goal
Qualitative and quantitative	To ensure implementation and replicability
Qualitative	To provide context and insight
Quantitative	To evaluate the effectiveness of evidence

For social science research to be funded and evaluated, the government and others have developed hierarchies of evidence with randomized controlled experiments being the gold standard, and the more times a study is replicated, the more reliable the finding.

The problem with that approach is that it may be untenable. It is easy to imagine running one cohort through a pilot versus a control group for a short period of time, but, ultimately, the reason the program is offered is to solve a problem, and saying that only 50 percent of employees will participate in a program to determine its efficacy may be a nonstarter with the business leader. It may win points among an editorial board or for tenure, but among CLOs, heads of talent, and business leaders who have P&L responsibility, this approach will, most often, be useless.

But as some of the lies have illustrated, in its absence, what has emerged is a system where evidence is largely word of mouth or personal testimonials, sometimes by vendors who have an agenda and sometimes by the learning professionals who have a point of view. These people act as advocates rather than researchers. As a result, much of what we design and deliver is rooted in little evidence that any of it works, but we have a large stake in saying it works, regardless of its actual efficacy.

However, we can't assume that learning professionals will always rise to the challenge. What is needed instead is a pragmatic solution. You must choose the level of sophistication you need to understand the impact of your programs. What tools can you use to gather evidence of impact? What tools do you use to analyze performance and learning?

We can address this issue pragmatically. In our country's courts, there are rules of evidence that dictate the way one gathers and analyzes evidence. For example, how DNA evidence is evaluated is different from how testimony is evaluated, but if both are gathered and evaluated accurately they can inform the jury. If someone provides testimony about events they witnessed while under the influence, or as someone who has failing eyesight, the testimony may be viewed differently. If DNA evidence has been tainted, it may be evaluated differently. In the same way, each of our disciplines have different research paradigms that cause us to approach evidence differently. This is how our systems align.

But the difference is in how the courts treat the evidence. There are different standards for evaluating the evidence, depending on whether the case is civil or criminal. In a criminal case, the standard is "beyond a reasonable doubt," whereas in a civil case, it is a "preponderance of evidence." You could present the same evidence, asking the same questions, and, depending on the standard, arrive at two different findings.

What we need is a way to evaluate evidence systematically, using a standard different from those used for tenure review or peer-reviewed journals. We need a preponderance of evidence standard that is quicker, more flexible, and easier to interpret than the research we do for our own education. And it needs to be driven by the needs of the market. The big data movement might make this fairly simple to execute in the near future.

We also need our profession to raise the bar. Some years ago, the Association for Talent Development was a major sponsor of a global initiative to create an ISO standard for corporate learning. While it was adopted by 42 countries, to my knowledge that standard was not adopted by a single U.S. employer. Our professional associations, particularly ATD, need to continue to lead the charge and call out the lies as they become clear.

What You Can Do in the Meantime

We continue to evolve as a profession. Hopefully, programs like the one I created at the University of Pennsylvania (PennCLO) and initiatives taken by organizations like ATD to develop professionals, can help establish a set of rules for research on learning. In the meantime, there are some pretty basic things you can do to catch lies and prevent lying.

Question everything. Be critical when you purchase and when you deliver. Be less of an advocate and more of a critic. And don't assume that because someone has a whitepaper or even one peer-reviewed article about her approach or product that it proves anything.

Research what you can. Not being able to run large-scale, longitudinal, controlled randomized trials with matched pairs is not an excuse to throw up your hands and follow the latest trend. Try to systematically question what you are planning and gather what evidence you can to support or refute what you actually do. And don't become so vested in a strategy that you ignore mounting evidence that what you are doing is having little effect.

Use empirically vetted content. In other words, if you have to choose between two marketing courses—one based on the research of a professor and the other one based on the whims of a prophet—go with the professor.

Use pedagogy aligned with your business problem. If you need to get your folks working better as virtual teams, a behaviorist approach may not be the most prudent design strategy.

If I've succeeded, I have raised more questions than I have answered and made you more skeptical than before. That is the crux of my message. Question everything to the extent possible and recognize that to be an effective professional you need to concurrently be a theoretician and researcher. While this is true in every profession, it is especially true in ours. Darwin argued eloquently for the survival of the fittest—that those species that could adapt would survive. For organizations, the only way to adapt is to learn. We are our companies' fulcrums to the future.

References

Browning, R. 1933. *Men and Women and Other Poems.* Boston: Orion Publishing Group.

Byrne, J.A. 2001. "The Real Confessions of Tom Peters." *Businessweek*, December 2. www.businessweek.com/stories/2001-12-02/the-real -confessions-of-tom-peters.

Collins, J. 2001. *Good to Great: Why Some Companies Make the Leap . . . and Others Don't.* New York: HarperBusiness.

Covey, S.R. 1989. *The Seven Habits of Highly Effective People.* New York: Free Press.

Gould, S.J. 1985. "The Median Isn't the Message." *Discover* (June): 40–42.

Peters, T.J., and R.H. Waterman Jr. 1982. *In Search of Excellence: Lessons From America's Best-Run Companies.* New York: Harper & Row.

3

More Lies About Instructional Design

Mindy Jackson

The truth about learning is that it's hard to create experiences that are relevant to diverse people. And supporting the transfer of learning is even harder. Our brains forget. The neurological mechanisms for memory encoding and retrieval require time and practice to develop our internal network of knowledge. And everyone's neural network—and its structures of mental schema—is unique to her experiences. Whether it's one-to-many training or one-to-one instruction, creating relevant and effective learning experiences is hard.

I try to be candid with what I know about learning. But some people don't want to listen to reality. They require immediate remedies to their performance and development needs. They seek expedient solutions, development shortcuts, and quick-acting salves. They want to believe that providing an annual 30-minute program on network security means that everyone logs off the computer before stepping away from their desks, or that an eight-hour seminar prepares the sales force for handling questions on new product features, or that two weeks of onboarding teaches the technician how to troubleshoot the breakage of a $1 million industrial machine. We know it requires more to transfer new skills and knowledge: continuing performance support, job aids, mentoring, access to experts and knowledge bases, performance plans and reviews, and so on.

Most lies about instructional design are but fantasies of an alternate reality—a truth we wish existed. The six lies exposed in this chapter result as much from self-deception as from a misunderstanding of the inextricable challenges of good instructional design.

Lie #1: A Good Training Program Will Solve the Problem

Attend training and voila! Go forth, lead, perform, and succeed.

A large multinational company wanted a high-quality 20-minute e-learning experience for its employees and customers. The topic was a new process innovation, and they had identified one learning objective: "to change the way the world does business." It was a terrific 20-minute program. Have you felt the change?

When pitching promises of a day-long transformative executive leadership program, a potential client asked me whether people should attend the program just once. I told the client yes, quickly adding that we hope the program is foundational to change and that you will follow up with support, incentives, and more training. It's difficult to defend the merits of a single training event having deep or lasting effect on your organization—and that's why training programs need to be designed with a longer view. One-and-done training is rarely a remedy, and often the problem, but it also can be part of an effective, broad-based solution.

Research from cognitive science validates the dulling effects of time (forgetting curves) and the strengthening of memory through spaced practice and repetition (spacing effect). Rather than cramming learning into a short time span, effective learning requires repeated exposure and practice over time. So a monthly seminar series or a set of e-learning courses, combined with performance support tools, is more effective than a one-shot approach.

Granted, there are times when you want a new learning program to start with intensity. That day-long transformative executive leadership program was meant to provide a sense of urgency, emotional motivation, and impact by catalyzing behavior change. It was an intense introduction to certain business problems and new ways of thinking about leading people to deal with these problems. It was an acceleration event, so follow-up and additional support is needed to sustain any change.

Inherent to the lie that one good training program can solve the problem is a self-deception akin to believing that drinking from a fire hose refreshes. Large amounts of content consumption do not equate to large amounts of learning transfer. Organizations thirst for the knowledge and skills their workforce needs to stay current and agile amid the fast-changing disruptions and innovations of business. When the need is now, it is human nature to seek shortcuts—often by trying to accomplish too much at once.

Providing learning—both formal training experiences and informal on-the-job experiences—and performance support requires a long-term view. Rather than thought of as peripheral occasions, learning and performance support yields the best results when integrated with the ecosystem of workplaces and work practices.

The truth is that learning requires more than one acquisition event. Evergreen knowledge and skills require continuing reinforcement and support.

Lie #2: ADDIE Is Dead

For a five-letter mnemonic device representing a process model, ADDIE (analysis → design → development → implementation → evaluation) sure receives a lot of criticism and hate. But try to think of any project that would not benefit from an inquisitive and iterative process model of define it, design it, make it, try it, and revise it. Alas, DDMTR is neither an attractive nor a memorable mnemonic. That is all ADDIE is—it's simply much easier to say, remember, and, apparently, hate. I hear complaints that ADDIE is not an agile and iterative development process. Whoever said ADDIE had to be strictly linear?

I recently completed a personal project that was an ADDIE process: creating a family photo album for my brother's birthday. I started by examining the boxes of photos inherited from our mother and sequencing the photos by time and event. I thought a lot about thematic representations and groupings of relatives we didn't know (how would I tell that part of the family story through the photos?). Next, I sampled some different patterns for page layouts and started placing the photos. I discovered new things I liked while working, so I made adjustments to previous pages. When I thought I was done, I looked over the entire book and then swapped several of the pages and photos around again. This is a simple example of ADDIE.

People say ADDIE takes too long. I finished my beautiful photo album in two days, and I'm happy with the results. Would I be as satisfied if I'd just put the pictures into the page sleeves without any forethought, organization, or trial and error? Certainly not. The process I used—simple and flexible—helped me create a better result.

The "ADDIE is dead" lie arises from a wish rather than a truth. Companies wish they could shorten the time to delivery by cutting analysis and design time and moving directly into development. Take the *A* for analysis and *D* for design away from ADDIE, and what is left? DIE. ADDIE is not dead; it's just been reduced to DIE. (How apropos for this new acronym.) But without analysis and design, the training is apt to fail. Engaging and effective learning programs come from informed and intentional design decisions. The best results are accomplished through purposeful planning and reasoned choices aligned to needs and goals. Isn't this true for any worthwhile project?

Rather than pushing learning projects toward best results, businesses too often place the imperative on driving projects to completion—often using artificial deadlines. My experience has been that timelines drive training development more than any other factor—and that rarely leads to the best possible outcome. In essence, there is an inverse relationship between the time spent on analysis and design and the level of risk associated with the initiative. As the amount of time spent increases, risk goes down; spend less time, and the risk goes (way) up.

In more than 20 years working as an instructional designer, I can only recall three large projects that were allocated enough time and resources for analysis and design. And those three are the best examples in my professional portfolio. They are my exemplars, not only because I was proud of the end products, but because they were also huge successes. Their success was validated by the satisfaction, performance gains, and the returns on investment the organizations saw. Two of the three returned more than $1 million in investment within six months of the program launch, and all were on time, on budget, and aligned to business objectives.

I don't understand what people mean when they say that Agile is a better development process than ADDIE. Agile development means tasks are broken into short phases of work that are assessed, adapted, and reassessed. The ADDIE process model is iterative and agile, and helps designers attend to the important components of instruction. It is scalable to any project budget, schedule, or scope. Its biggest challenge is the lack of flexibility in those who use it. The methodology doesn't dictate rigid linearity. That comes from users who don't think about how ADDIE can be best used to solve instructional or performance problems.

Lie #3: Mobile Is the Killer App for Training

Mobile devices are fantastic tools for training and development. Laptops, tablets, and smartphones all enable mobile learning. If the tool is portable and accessible anytime, it can be called a mobile device. That's why books and training manuals also can be categorized as mobile. But when customers ask for a mobile solution, they're usually referring to handheld telecommunication devices.

I love the story from John Seely Brown, former chief scientist of Xerox Corporation and director of its Palo Alto Research Center, about providing mobile phones to Xerox service repair technicians (many years before cell-phones were commodities). At Xerox, a reorganization separated technicians accustomed to co-location and social access to one another. They regularly shared field experiences and war stories about managing machine breakdowns and customers nearing meltdowns. Not only had they formed a community of practice, according to Brown, but their informal mentoring and workplace learning had boosted problem identification and reduced repair times. Once separated, field performance dropped. Mobile phones thus reconnected the technicians to their community of practice.

Mobile is an anywhere, anytime access technology. Mobile can tether us to social networks, information hubs, knowledge management systems, just-in-time training, and other forms of performance support. But is mobile the killer app for training?

With HTML5 and responsive design guidelines, webpages can scale for legibility on different screen dimensions, like a 25-inch computer monitor or a four-inch phone screen. But the affordances of extreme screen scalability are mostly forgotten by customers who want their employees to be able to take a training program on their phones—while waiting for airplanes, eating a sandwich, or waiting for a meeting. Just because the training can be delivered to a mobile device does not mean it will deliver the same quality experience on all mobile devices.

Enspire, the company for which I work, mostly creates immersive learning experiences that put the learner in simulations of real-world contexts and within interactive case studies. Sure, simulations can be delivered on a small screen, but the size limits the realism and depth of interactions. Notice how most games played on cell phones are based on patterns and repetitive movements within abstract environments. Finer and nuanced details are sacrificed for usability within the constricted screen space.

Often we put technology to the wrong purposes when we use a tool in ways that don't match its natural affordances. An affordance is a quality of an object that provides useful interaction with the object, such as a doorknob to be twisted and a door handle to be pushed or pulled. I like the analogy of a pencil: It's a great tool for writing on paper, but not such a good tool for punching holes into paper. You can do it, but the holes are apt to be ragged and misaligned. That's an example of a technology being extended beyond the affordances of its design—beyond its purpose.

Mobile has many uses for training and development, especially for just-in-time resources and performance support. But it can be misused as well. Sadly, mobile's quintessential affordance—social access—is mostly underused by learning and development. As the Xerox repair technicians' story showed, mobile is a killer app for accessing expertise in your organization. As a social learning tool, mobile can accelerate learning curves, expand knowledge sharing, increase the uptake of process norms, and support a connected community of practice within your organization. Mobile can expand the reach of your training and learning programs, but it is often not the best choice for delivering your training and learning experiences.

Lie #4: Big Data Analytics Provide Adaptive Learning

Don't be fooled by the grand pronouncements (and buzzwords) that big data analytics will revolutionize instruction. This lie is based on high hopes that data analytics will result in more personal and relevant instructional experiences, while overlooking the enormous hurdles to implementation.

Data analytics have been effective tools for business planning, especially for sales and marketing. But the proof cases for data-driven learning analytics are nascent. To be sure, I'm optimistic. Imagine a future in which data-driven instruction personalizes and adapts learning in real time, based on individual differences and preferences. That's the true promise of computer-based instruction. But let's move beyond the speculative to what is known and doable today.

Here are the broad basics of what I know about data analytics. Collecting data provides a record of past events. By analyzing these data, we can tell a story about the past. And by using algorithms—based on statistical inference models—we can then calculate probabilities.

But what else is required to yield useful meaning from data analytics? Consider data collection. How confident are you in the reliability and validity of the data you collected? Do the data points you tagged consistently and accurately measure the skill, knowledge, or behavior you intended to measure? We can drown ourselves in data points from click-streams. The story you get from the data depends on the data selected and on the suppositions you made about the data's value. It's a sticky proposition, but it gets even stickier.

Now consider what must happen within the "black box" to extrapolate data into an adaptive learning path (Figure 3-1). We know the operations within the black box present several difficult engineering problems. The system must somehow generate a path based on the statistical inferences of past data, the learner's knowledge and skills, and correlate instructional goals to available curriculum. To do this, the system will require learning maps (canonical knowledge structures that trace skill enablers and knowledge dependencies), accurate learner profiles of present-state needs, and rules of logic (Bayesian networks) to reconcile the multiple inputs.

Figure 3-1. Black Box

I use the black box analogy so we don't have to concern ourselves with its internal workings. Suffice it to say, serious consideration and effort are required for data inputs. So let's look at the other side of the equation. What does the black box produce? Learning analytics? Branching through instructional assets? A curricular sequence?

No. The black box doesn't output curriculum and instruction; rather, it calculates probabilities as outputs (if-then-else logic). At best, we might say the system recommends a pathway based on the input data points and their correlations. You, or your instructional design team, must develop all the instructional activities for creating adaptive paths. Think about how much training is required to create skill and knowledge paths based on individual differences. Think about an adaptive system reacting appropriately to 30, 300, or 3,000 employees.

With data we can make better decisions. With data we can be more responsive to individual and group needs. And with data we can identify opportunities to improve or optimize instructional pathways. The lie I'm attempting to dispel is the hyperbole of big data learning analytics or that big data is an easy, or even sufficient, solution to providing adaptive learning. Beyond the data—and a brilliant statistician, of course—are colossal requirements: learner profiles, learning maps, data reliability and validity testing, and multiple curricula and instructional pathways. Someone has to make it all; it doesn't come in a box.

Lie #5: Khan Is King: Long Live Content Curation

Khan Academy is a fabulous online repository of learning objects, as well as full-fledged curricula and instructional pathways that addresses many subjects. (Note: Khan Academy is making progress with using big data analytics for adaptive learning pathways for math and science learning objectives by analyzing use patterns and generating knowledge maps from its millions of online users.) The open educational resources movement provides unprecedented access to share, use, and reuse high-quality training materials. But when I hear suggestions that content curators are replacing instructional designers, I want to yell back: "What about your context?" And so the age-old debate continues between content and context.

Indeed, there are many opportunities for content curation, such as using open-source content to target foundational knowledge and skills. For instance, a nonfinancial manager needs to understand how to read P&L spreadsheets and calculate cash flow statements. Khan Academy has training videos about that. But the curated content does not offer anything on how your company shares costs among its departments.

Take another example. A sales team seeks to improve performance. It finds a free, online sales cycle management program. An excellent find. The course provides an orientation to the seven stages of the sales cycle. But that course is not going to teach the ins and outs of the team's products, services, or vision of the customer experience. Many of the training parts can be cobbled together from multiple sources. Perhaps it's a bit disjointed from the team's own business context, but it can work for some uses.

Regardless, most organizational training needs revolve around the intricate details of your business processes, customer needs, and supply chain partners. Even with the off-the-shelf resources, your organization needs instructional designers to gather requirements, conduct task analysis, establish learning goals and objectives, locate or create the instructional materials and performance support, and much more.

I'm excited by the prospects of content curation combined with crowd-sourcing. In this way, content vetting could be done on a larger scale, with employees rating the usefulness of instructional materials. With an eye on the context of their own daily work and learning needs, employees could filter out irrelevant content pieces and bring forth the best. The truth is, context matters.

Lie #6: People Learn Differently Now

I'm often asked how instructional technologies are changing the way people learn. Sometimes my first, and rather coy, response is: "Not much at all." Human brains function today just as they did 10,000 years ago.

The internal mechanisms of human learning and memory have not suddenly evolved. Today's generation doesn't learn differently from previous generations. What is different, however, are innovative instructional technologies and a better understanding of human cognition. The strategies and tools for supporting learning and memory are rapidly changing.

So it's a wonderful time to be in training and education. Great new tools permeate the classroom and the workplace. In fact, the influx of new educational technology products—podcasts, Twitter, motion graphics, games, simulations, social networks, social collaboration, intranets, hangouts, wikis, Wikipedia, e-books—makes choosing which ones to use daunting, but exhilarating. Some are new, some are different, and some are not. People may not learn all that differently today, but we certainly have more choices for access points and instructional methods.

From K–12 and postsecondary teachers, I often hear stories of tablet technologies and audience response systems flipping the classroom from content-centric to learner-centric experiences. Project-based learning and peer instruction are widely adopted in our best universities.

Michael Starbird, a brilliant mathematician and teacher at the University of Texas at Austin, told me that too many instructional activities and too much classroom time is devoted to getting to the right answer. He suggests that we focus on investigating mistakes and raising essential questions about a problem. Studies show that this teaching strategy—productive failure—draws learner attention to critical features and leads to enduring understanding far better than direct instruction.

People are not learning differently; we are teaching more effectively.

Conclusion

In *Lies About Learning*, I wrote a chapter rebuking the lies that devalued instructional design as a process discipline:

> ➤ Instructional design is irrelevant.

> ➤ All you need is a subject matter expert.

➤ Instructional design is a front-end process only.

➤ Instructional design takes too long and costs too much.

➤ Instructional design makes learning tedious and not very fun.

➤ Instructional design is out of touch with the dynamics of business.

This time I've written about the common lies I hear from clients and learning industry pundits. I bet you've heard them too:

➤ A good training program will solve the problem.

➤ ADDIE is dead.

➤ Mobile is the killer app for training.

➤ Big data analytics provide adaptive learning.

➤ Khan is king: Long live content curation.

➤ People learn differently now.

These lies, and many others, continue to proliferate due to misconceptions and misinformation from people with their own agendas, often related to selling a product. Allocating the time and resources to instructional design provides the best opportunity for delivering effective learning and performance improvements. To think otherwise is to indulge in fantasy or denial.

Human resource development should not happen on the periphery—it belongs within the ecosystem of the enterprise to provide and sustain learning, collaborative social experiences, and performance support. With new technologies, better instructional methods, and scientific insights into human learning, instructional design can, and should, lead the way.

Part II

Lies About the Business and Management of Learning

4

Lies About Managing the Learning Function

Edward A. Trolley

Sixteen years ago, David van Adelsberg and I wrote *Running Training Like a Business* because we were hearing the same concerns about training from senior executives with whom we spoke, and we were seeing the same structural and financial challenges with training at companies with which we interacted (van Adelsberg and Trolley 1999).

At that time, many training organizations had large staffs and large fixed costs. Training groups were pervasive across the organizations, and they were doing their own thing. So consistency was lacking, quality uneven, and spending underleveraged. Training professionals were domain oriented, not business oriented; they were focused on building their own programs, not on finding the best possible solution. Success was measured by volume—classes, courses, and training days—rather than by value. Vendors were accessing organizations anywhere they could get in and through as many people as they could find. Some training programs were delivering questionable value and focused on activity instead of application. Organizations took no real stewardship over training, relegating it to a "backroom" activity—a significant, but difficult to quantify, cost. They did not view training as strategically linked to business.

As a result, executives did not know how much they were spending on training, nor could they articulate the business value they were getting from their training investments. And they often thought training organizations were out of the loop, operating separately from the business. These executives saw a widening gap between the skills their businesses required and the skills the workforce actually showed. They saw training as part of the employee contract and a good thing to do for employees, but believed the investment–value equation was broken.

Today's Reality

Fast forward to 2015. Is the training industry really all that different than it was 16 years ago? Certainly. We've had to figure out how to design and to deliver training differently. We've also had to figure out how to use technology differently. We've had to figure out how to use blended learning, mobile technology, simulations, gamification, social platforms, performance support systems, and talent management systems. More learning is being done informally than formally. Industry professionals are using new buzzwords. Learners have changed, technology has changed, tools have changed, the business and competitive environment have changed, and budgets have changed. The list goes on.

But what hasn't changed? How we manage training. When it comes to managing training, the more things change, the more they stay the same. In fact, the list of what hasn't changed when it comes to managing the learning function is pretty long.

In 2011, NIIT, a leading supplier of training services, commissioned Corporate University Exchange (CorpU) to conduct research to see how companies were performing against the key tenants of *Running Training Like a Business*. NIIT wanted to find out if the concepts were still valid, given that the book was written more than a decade previously. Studying more than 150 companies, CorpU found that only 18 were high-performers in running training like a business, measured primarily by whether they delivered quantifiable value to the business (CorpU 2011). That is not much different from the situation in 1999, and this is why I contend that the more things change, the more they stay the same. From this research, CorpU put forth five must-dos for effective training organizations:

> ➤ run at the speed of business
> ➤ be lean and agile
> ➤ ensure a laser-focus on business (to drive business value)
> ➤ provide data-driven analytics (to prove business value)
> ➤ drive innovation.

To what degree are you doing these five things? How are you making them happen? This is not rocket science. Successful business must take these actions each and every day.

In 1999, we said that the beginning of the beginning, the first critical step, is getting connected to the business—what we called *business linkage*. We meant that training had to become laser-focused on what's important to the business and provide learning solutions that advanced the business's goals and objectives. If not done correctly, nothing else would really matter. The training on which companies spend so much money would be irrelevant. Businesspeople would look at training as a cost, not an investment. Training professionals would forever be on the outside looking in on business discussions. And of course if times got tough, training would be at the top of the list for cutting costs.

Sixteen years ago, we offered guidance on how to strengthen business linkages, but it remains a significant issue for too many training organizations. Business leaders continue to question the value they receive from their very large investments in training. At a recent conference I attended, a panel of CLOs scoffed at the idea that they needed a seat at the business table, suggesting that way of thinking has passed. But those days are not over. It is even more critical today that training becomes intimate with business and delivers the value that warrants an invitation to conversations among business executives.

If we are going to build the business linkages we need to be successful, we must:

> Create roles in our training organizations that interact continually and consistently with business executives.

> Train the people in these roles to engage in meaningful business conversations with their customers, using questions that elicit actionable information.

> Know the expectations of business executives and whether we are meeting them.

> Assess and document the capabilities required to meet business objectives, quantify the gaps in capabilities, and design strategies that can close the gaps.

Let's not offer 1,000 e-learning courses that no one uses, ask businesspeople what training they need (when they should be looking to us to help them figure it out), or assume that training is the only solution. In other words, let's be businesspeople in training, not training people in business.

Managing (Formal) Learning

Everyone is talking about 70-20-10 these days. Agree or disagree with the ratio, what is hard to disagree with is that a lot of learning happens informally. But companies still spend more than $200 billion on formal learning each year. The questions, then, are: How well are we managing formal learning? Do we really know how much we are spending, what we are spending it on, what we are getting for it, or if it is aligned to the business? Do executives understand the business value they are getting? All indications suggest that we don't have good answers to these questions.

Every day we see companies trying to get a better handle on how much they are spending and the value they are getting in return. But at the same time, we see companies with highly decentralized models, where training happens everywhere, that say they don't really care if the same vendor is being used for the same programs in different parts of the organization, or if the company is being charged different fees for the same content. We also see different vendors offering the same types of programs, but with inconsistent content, uneven quality, and, of course, wildly different pricing.

And then there is training administration. Large companies have full-time teams devoted to providing training administration, as well as numerous part-time training administrators across the organization. In many cases, higher-paid learning professionals spend some 30–50 percent of their time performing administrative tasks. Training administration is a critically important, but low-value-added, activity. It consumes human and financial resources. We need to figure out how to do this largely transactional work differently to reduce costs, free up key resources, and improve overall quality and control.

Delivering or facilitating training is also undermanaged. Many employees do this as a small part of their jobs. They may be technical experts and top performers, but that does not necessarily make them good teachers. Facilitation is a professional craft. Why trust it to people who are not experts? It is not unusual for learning leaders to say that they use full-time trainers less than 50 percent of the time. (I recently talked with a learning leader who said she uses full-time trainers less than 20 percent of the time.) So, once again, are you managing learning as effectively as you could?

And, finally, how are you managing custom content development? Do you have a staff of instructional designers and content developers? Are they professionally trained, or did you find them from somewhere else in the organization because they were available? Are you holding yourself to the same standard that business leaders would hold the chief information officer for having staff with deep, relevant technical expertise? These are the questions you should be asking as you evaluate how you are managing the learning function.

As a training leader, if you are not looking for ways to continually improve effectiveness and efficiency, and you are not open to new and different ways to increase value, reduce cost, move fixed costs to variable costs, and gain access to better capability, you are not serving your company to the best of your ability. I encourage you to step back, take a hard look at what you are doing and how you are doing it, identify options for you to improve, evaluate those options, build business cases, and then make decisions that benefit your company.

At a learning conference I recently attended, one speaker said that the work we are doing in learning is serving a noble cause. And I agree. But unless we are helping our company be more competitive and productive, grow at a rate that business executives expect, give employees the skills they need to be more effective, or reduce costs and provide unmistakable value to customers, our work may also be irrelevant. The days of training being a good thing to do are no longer enough for business executives. When they see large sums of money invested in training, but are unsure of the value they are receiving in return, they are sometimes left no choice but to move investments elsewhere.

Measuring Value and Impact

How do you respond when someone asks you about measuring the value of training? It's too hard. It can't be done. There are too many factors. We can't quantify the value. It costs too much. We can use other indicators instead of hard business measures. These are simply not acceptable answers. Let's look at what business executives say. A 2009 ROI Institute study found that:

> ➤ 96 percent of executives want to see the business impact of learning, yet only 8 percent receive it now.

> ➤ 74 percent of executives want to see ROI data, but only 4 percent have it now.

Do we really think our responses are acceptable? Our business executives certainly don't. If we continue to ignore or sidestep this measurement question, we are destined to be the first to go when times get tough.

Let's end this debate and start doing the heavy lifting to define the quantifiable business value we deliver from our work. Let's understand what our customers need. Let's ensure that we understand how they will measure success (the measurements they think are important) before we begin to do the work. Let's define the factors that could impact the results. And then let's help our customers measure the value against the measures they defined at the beginning.

The ROI Institute study said that business executives want hard evidence. So let's give it to them, because without it, we give them no choice but to conclude that there is no evidence.

A Different Perspective

Over the years I have written about, talked about, and debated what I believe are the essential leadership actions we must take to dramatically move the needle on how we manage training and how we drive transformation. While it is hard work, and it might require that you think differently about things, I believe that we must transform (Table 4-1).

Table 4-1. Change in Perspective for Learning Leaders

From	To
Training department	Training enterprise
Cost of training	Investment in learning
Attendees or participants	Customers
Measuring activity	Measuring results
What training you need	What business problem you are trying to solve
Training as the end result	Business outcomes as the end result
Mastering content	Improving performance
Allocation of expense	Pay for use
Activity	Application
Smile sheets	Customer success

While one could argue that Table 4-1 oversimplifies things and suggests that the columns are "either/or" instead of "and," the point is that we must start to think differently about the work we do.

Most importantly, while we all agree that developing employees continues to be both critically important and the right thing to do, the context has to be about delivering real business value. Training's feel good charter is out of date (and has been for a while), and business executives expect more.

Why now? As someone once said: "It's the economy, stupid!" And that was before the recent economic downturn. Never before have the pressures been so intense. Every day, we see increased pressure on:

➤ CEOs, executives, and business leaders to deliver more revenue, higher earnings, and greater shareholder value

➤ functional (nonrevenue producing) organizations, including HR, to demonstrate impact and value

➤ learning and development to demonstrate their relevance almost daily, reduce costs, and dramatically improve measurable impact.

And never before has the business case been stronger and the mandate clearer, as indicated by the 15th Annual PwC Global CEO Survey, which stated:

> More CEOs are changing talent management strategies than, for example, adjusting approaches to risk: 23 percent expect "major change" to the way they manage their talent. And skills shortages are seen as top threat to business expansion. . . . One in four CEOs said they were unable to pursue a market opportunity or have had to cancel or delay a strategic initiative because of talent. One in three is concerned that skills shortages impacted their company's ability to innovate effectively. (PwC 2012, 20)

Actions We Should Take

It's easy to talk about all the problems and challenges and to ask: "What should we do?" Here are some transformational steps that learning leaders should seriously consider.

Conduct a business assessment of training. This means far more than confirming the professional competency of the training staff, measuring activity levels, or even documenting that skills are being applied on the job. It means assessing the strategic and financial return earned on the training investment. It means looking at everything—people, products, processes, technology, and customer satisfaction and value being delivered. Doug Howard, CEO of Training Industry, predicted that:

> Learning leaders will seek objective assessment of the training organization. . . . [They] will be conducting—using both internal and external resources—objective assessments of their training department readiness. . . . Companies that make the most of these assessments will be those that are most willing to open themselves to an honest evaluation (warts and all). (Howard 2010)

Understand the expectations of business executives. This is not about what training business executives need but, instead, what they expect from you—how you work with them, how you interact with their organizations, the services they value, how they expect you to deliver them, and the value expectations they have for the investments they are making. I have found that the list of expectations from senior business executives is not long, and they can articulate the list very crisply. But you have to ask. You have to engage them in a serious discussion on this topic. Understanding these expectations and asking for candid feedback about your performance will provide you with valuable information to evaluate where you are today and what you can improve in the future.

Manage your costs to acceptable levels and always consider the value you are delivering. Cost management will always be a priority for training organizations. But costs will be a more visible and serious issue when the value you are delivering is not evident. Having said that, we still need to be great stewards of the investment we receive from the business and we need to ensure that we are operating at an optimal cost level. Here are five critical actions managing costs effectively:

➤ Know how much your company is spending on training, where it is going, and what it is being spent on.

➤ Continually look for opportunities to move fixed costs to variable costs. This is important because it allows us to pay for what we use, scale up and down without having to hire or fire, and eliminate the unpopular allocation model for spreading training costs.

➤ Uncover the hidden training costs. For example, if you use outside providers, there are costs associated with each step in the procurement process. How much does it cost you to pay an invoice? How many invoices do you process in a month? How much time are your training professionals spending in the vendor procurement process? How many corporate resources are spending some part of their time doing training-related activities?

➤ Take aggressive actions to reduce costs. Use outsourcing wherever possible because you will reap the benefits of your outsourcing provider's best practice processes, ability to leverage resources, and off-shoring when possible.

➤ Manage the total cost of training, not just the direct, out-of-pocket costs. Figure 4-1 illustrates the elements of total cost, most of which are often overlooked.

Figure 4-1. Training Cost Model

My research has shown that the total cost of training is anywhere from three to five times more than the direct costs. That is significant because it offers many opportunities to reduce the hidden indirect costs and thus have a significant business impact. If you can reduce the length of a program or set of programs, you can reduce both delivery expense and participant labor costs associated with training. And by reducing the length of the training, you are returning people to their jobs sooner, which has a positive impact on productivity. Managing the total cost of training leads you to very different decisions than if you are just managing the direct costs. Training organizations should report on the total cost of training and the influence they are having on it in a timely basis. We should not be afraid to take credit for being effective stewards of organizational assets.

Training has characteristics that don't support high fixed costs. Training is cyclical, as the demand for it ebbs and flows. While some of the work training organizations do remains predictable and consistent, like most businesses there are peaks and valleys. Staffing for the peaks is expensive and risky.

Training is far too often viewed as discretionary. In organizations in which training leaders have not presented a clear and compelling business case for their existence, training functions are one of the first to be asked to downsize in a challenging business environment.

Scalability is important. Because training demand can be variable, the best-managed organizations have the ability to scale up and down. This means having ready access to qualified training professionals who can quickly supplement the fixed staff when demand exceeds capacity, and being able to reduce resources when capacity exceeds demand.

Outsourcing

So far I have suggested that training organizations would be far better off if they shift from a highly fixed cost structure to one that is more flexible. As a result, outsourcing is a serious alternative for training leaders. But training leaders are still hesitant to treat it as a viable option; another thing that hasn't changed during the past 16 years. Here are the five most common lies about outsourcing.

Lie #1: Outsourcing Can't Reduce Costs

Talk about extremes. How can we be so far apart on the important issue of whether outsourcing can reduce costs? It is amazing that this debate continues. But perhaps it's not a debate. Perhaps, at least from the training leaders' side of the aisle, it's more of a smokescreen.

In general, outsourcing has been shown to reduce costs across various functions, including information technology, human resources, and finance and accounting. For example, HR outsourcers are confident in their ability to reduce costs because the work they take on is mostly, if not completely, transactional, such as benefits administration and payroll processing (HR is estimated to be 70 percent transactional and 30 percent strategic), and it benefits from leverage, scale, and common processes and technologies. And outsourcing gets even better if the outsourcer can provide services to its clients using a variable cost model, so that the clients do not have to carry high fixed costs and can pay on a per-transaction basis for the services as they use them. Research reports and case studies on this are pretty consistent: Outsourcing reduces costs. While some outsourcing relationships have failed to meet expectations of cost reduction, quality improvement, and better control, industry experts and advisers would say that is the exception rather than the rule.

But here is the issue with training. Unlike these other transaction-heavy activities, training is roughly 30 percent transactional and 70 percent strategic, and unlike payroll, benefits, and other HR services, it is highly discretionary. So if cost reductions are the key driver, just stop training altogether or reduce the volume. As I suggested earlier, the key issue is that the investment–value equation for training is broken in many organizations, so any training outsourcing must be driven by the need to increase value.

Training outsourcers—particularly those who take on the transactional elements of training, such as technology, administration, and vendor management—can reduce the cost of these activities because they, like their counterparts in other functions, benefit from scale, leverage, and common technology and processes. Cost reduction is necessary, but it's not sufficient. And while it might buy you some time, failure to address the value side of the equation will still leave you vulnerable to questions from business executives.

So back to the big question: Does training outsourcing reduce costs? The answer is that it does in transactional areas and it may in the more strategic areas, such as content development and delivery. Overall, the goal should be a reduction in the unit cost of training (the costs per person per hour, day, or year). In fact, when we dramatically improve the value of training, companies actually tend to spend more, not less.

Lie #2: No Outsider Can Know My Business Like I Do

Doubting the know-how of outsiders is another objection raised by internal training resources. Outsourcing does not mean that you stop accessing the subject matter expertise of your businesses. It means that you start accessing resources that are professional, skilled, trained, experienced, and best-in-class in doing what they do. Companies have been outsourcing or out-tasking various parts of training for years, particularly to gain access to content. That is why there is such a huge market for training companies. These companies work with their customers, both training professionals and subject matter experts, to put together learning solutions that directly address business needs. These companies understand how to design, develop, and deliver training, and they apply those capabilities to the subject matter or business issues at hand. Even the skeptics who say, "no outsider can know my business like I do," frequently tap into these providers for help.

Training outsourcers possess the same capabilities as internal training organizations. Not only do they have access to training expertise, they understand processes, operations, and technology. They integrate these capabilities to serve their customers. I would argue that the only proprietary aspect of any business is the subject matter. All the surrounding training processes—design, development, delivery, technology, administration, vendor management, and others—are fairly generic and certainly aren't compromised by the outsourcing provider "not knowing your business."

Lie #3: Strategic Activities Can't Be Outsourced

Training leaders—and training outsourcers who don't offer the services and thus argue that they should not be outsourced—perpetuate the myth that strategic activities can't be outsourced. The most strategic of training activities is understanding the business's direction, strategy, challenges, issues, objectives, and goals, and then determining how and where training can add value. Some people call this activity performance consulting; I prefer relationship management. Relationship managers understand their customer's business, live inside the business, sit at the business table, look for ways in which their work can make a difference, and bring broad business insights to their customers. They understand when training can help and when it can't. They don't ask businesspeople: "What training do you need?" Instead, they talk about what the sales or market share or productivity improvement objectives are and present options for advancing them through training, performance support, or any other service a highly skilled training organization can provide.

Several years ago I did a training outsourcing deal in which my customer wanted to retain the relationship management role. We set up the operational process so that the customer's employees would work with their internal clients and then work with my company to deliver solutions.

Within short order, the training leader for this company received calls from senior business leaders demanding to know: "What's new about this? These are the same people who have not served my business well in the past. You promised me transformation with this outsourcing initiative, not more of the same!" Suffice it to say, the training leader acted quickly and added this work to the contract. My firm brought in a team that was highly skilled in this type of business consulting. The training leader changed his approach, and the business benefited.

It is understandable why internal training employees might argue against outsourcing this part of the training value chain. But why do so many training outsourcers agree? There are two major reasons: First, they see their business as transactional, not transformational. As a result, they don't have a service offering that extends across the entire training value chain. Instead, they focus solely on the transactional elements. And second, they don't want to create conflict with a potential client for fear of losing their chance at the opportunity. Isn't the client always right? But providers who always agree with you are not providing the kind of insight, expertise, and know-how that you are paying for and that you deserve.

Lie #4: People Don't Lose Their Jobs After Outsourcing

I have been on many panels with outsourcing providers that say that training professionals don't lose their jobs in an outsourcing model. We need to stop sugarcoating this. The entry point for most training outsourcers is cost reduction, and most research indicates that the primary reason to outsource is to reduce operating costs. It is hard to reduce costs without eliminating jobs. It is that simple. Outsourcers who are not explicit about this are either ignoring the issue or being less than truthful. I hasten to add that if cost is, in fact, an issue and you don't outsource, it is likely that jobs will still be lost, but the numbers may be higher.

Lie #5: Outsourcing Means Losing Control

The idea that outsourcing means losing control couldn't be further from the truth. In fact, I would contend that you really don't have control now. In many organizations, training continues to be one of the largest unmanaged expenses. Training is pervasive. It happens everywhere. And most of the costs occur outside HR. Organizations have multiple systems, processes, and people engaged in the design, development, and delivery of training. But very few organizations know how much they are really spending, and, as a result, they have little control over the investment.

If you outsource in a comprehensive way, you should work with your partner to identify how much is being spent; where it is being spent; what processes, technology, and people are being used; where duplication and redundancy exist; and so on. And when your partner works with you to manage all aspects of the training value chain in an integrated way, your company will have a single point of accountability with service-level agreements, management of costs and quality, and, most important, control.

On both sides of the outsourcing table, I have seen control increase dramatically through the process. And that holds true regardless of the scope of the outsourcing arrangement. Being able to look to a single point of control for accountability, metrics, responsibility, and costs is a significant benefit of the outsourcing decision.

Conclusion

In this chapter, I have attempted to address many of the lies, myths, and beliefs about managing the learning function. I have discussed some misconceptions about outsourcing, the need to focus on efficiency and effectiveness, how to gain control over the training value chain, and how and why we must think about managing the training function like it is a business. Our measures should be related to the business of training and the work of training. Customer retention, cycle time, quality, costs, and customer expectations are as important as the first three levels of the

Kirkpatrick measurement model. And at the end of the day, the only true measure is the business value your customer receives from the investment in you. That is what businesses worry about, and that is what training professionals at all levels should fixate on. Our success, as with any business, should be measured by the success of our customers. And always remember, it's not about training; it's about results.

References

CorpU. 2011. *Running Training Like a Business: 2011 Research Update.* Mechanicsburg, PA: CorpU.

Howard, D. 2010. "10 Predictions for 2010: Will It Be the Year for Real Change?" *Training Industry*, January 12. www.trainingindustry.com /articles/10-predictions-for-2010.aspx.

PwC. 2012. *Delivering Results: Growth and Value in a Volatile World* (15th Annual Global CEO Survey 2012). www.pwc.com/gx/en/ceo-survey /pdf/15th-global-pwc-ceo-survey.pdf.

van Adelsberg, D., and E.A. Trolley. 1999. *Running Training Like a Business.* San Francisco: Berrett-Koehler.

5

Lies About Learning to Lead

Terry Traut

T here are three types of lies: lies, damned lies, and statistics." This quote by Mark Twain, who attributed it to British prime minister Benjamin Disraeli, forms the basis of this chapter on lies about learning to lead:

➤ Learning to lead people is easy—that's the lie.

➤ I don't need leadership development because I'm already a good leader—that's the damned lie.

➤ I subscribe to the [pick a leadership guru or program] approach of leadership—that's the statistically short-lived delusion.

This chapter is about learning to lead. I'll discuss the lies some leaders use to avoid leadership development and what we, as proponents of effective leadership and as training practitioners, can do to help leaders learn to lead and manage people effectively.

Lie #1: Lie—Learning to Lead Is Easy

Let's face it—leading is not easy. For many of us it's not natural. In fact, for many of us in leadership positions, leadership wasn't a career choice or something we considered majoring in at college. Most of us who have assumed—or been bestowed—a leadership position probably stood out for being great autonomous, independent contributors or for being more technically capable and harder working than our peers. One day we got promoted, and we suddenly found ourselves with the title of team leader or supervisor and thought in our naïve, unknowing way: "How hard can this leadership stuff be? It must be easy! If those people [pointing upward in hierarchy] can do it, surely I can do it as well."

Well, leading may be simple, but it's certainly not easy. Why? Because the characteristics that made us successful and helped us earn that promotion are not necessarily what's needed to be a good leader, according to Marshall Goldsmith, co-author of *What Got You Here Won't Get You There* (2007). In fact, they are likely to make the transition to leadership more difficult.

Leaders have to get things done through others, so their individual technical prowess, attitude, and drive doesn't matter nearly as much as that of the team. In truth, it's likely that few employees can match the new leader's capabilities or passion for the work. That's probably why the leader was promoted in the first place and his peers weren't. But many new leaders end up alienating their teams out of frustration over what is perceived as a lack of skill or initiative. Or they may simply end up doing the work themselves, since no one can do it as well or as fast as they can. More often than not, this leads to failure as a leader.

Helping teams develop, engage, and perform is what new leaders are all about now. But no one ever (or rarely) takes first-time leaders aside and shows them how to lead. No one ever tells them that their individual skills, which made them what they are today, are no longer as important— that getting others to excel is now what matters.

The shift in what skills are important is often the greatest hurdle leaders face—and what we in leadership development must first, and continuously, address. Making this shift is akin to looking at one of those 3-D pictures. With concentrated effort—and a bit of squinting—you might be able to tease the 3-D picture of dolphins or a cityscape from the abstract. Then poof, the 3-D image is gone. Shifting a new leader's perspective about what is now important is equally challenging, but it is the necessary first step in development.

The shift occurs at each transition in a leader's journey up the organizational ladder, as Ram Charan and his co-authors point out in *The Leadership Pipeline: How to Build the Leadership Powered Company* (2007). From supervisor of individual contributors to manager of managers to business unit leader to C-level leader, each transition first requires a shift in values and in what is important for success in each role.

There are two main reasons why learning to lead is not easy: First, learning to lead initially requires unlearning. And second, leading is a messy business.

"But how hard can it be?" you ask. "I've seen people lead; I've been led." That's the equivalent of saying: "I can be an effective parent because I was a kid once." Not true.

Learning to lead requires rewiring the brain. It requires that leaders unlearn many of the behaviors that have become engrained in who they are. Leaders can't rely on technical ability; they must ensure that their teams have the technical capabilities they need to succeed. Leaders can no longer rely on their own initiative to carry the day; they need to inspire and motivate others to demonstrate the initiative and drive their teams' need to achieve their collective goals. Leaders no longer have the luxury of managing just themselves and their own little quirks; they are now responsible for dealing with the quirks and idiosyncrasies of their direct reports. That's a messy, complicated thing.

And guess what. Most new leaders inherit teams hired by someone else. Messy. And many leaders were part of the team they now manage. Doubly so.

Leading would be easier if it weren't for the people. And learning to lead, by extension, would also be a piece of cake. Unfortunately, it's filled with all the messiness and unpredictability that comes from working with people. And that's also what makes leading, which is arguably the most fulfilling job in the world, so difficult—if it were easy, anyone could do it.

And so that is why leadership development is so important. We all have thoughts about what it takes to lead—"I need to be strong," "I need to be charismatic," "I need to have the answers"—and many of them are simply wrong.

In the end, effective leaders must:

> **Link organizational goals to individual contributions.** Effective leaders need to ensure that their employees know that what they do is meaningful and how it contributes to the greater good.

> **Support people as they contribute to organizational goals.** Sometimes this support can be a pat on the back or a kick in the pants. Sometimes it's recognizing when to train employees and when to offer feedback, coaching, or stretch assignments. There are thousands of ways to provide support, and effective leaders need to know them all. This is what makes leading challenging—and rewarding.

> **Connect with people.** Effective leaders must be seen as authentic and trustworthy—and secure in their roles. Connecting with people not only builds human capital and trust, but it also enables work to get done.

> **Delegate effectively.** Effective leaders need to delegate—not only to get work done, but also to develop the skills and confidence of team members. New leaders often struggle with delegating, thinking that it is easier and faster to do the work themselves. Not true. Leaders need to delegate the appropriate responsibility—ensuring that the person has a good chance of succeeding, while not putting the team at risk.

> **Have the tough conversations when needed.** And by extension, do so in a way that improves performance and increases loyalty and commitment. When team members know that their leader cares about them and their performance, team effectiveness skyrockets. Strong leaders emerge when confronted with challenges.

For the most part, everything leaders do is in support of these five competencies. So leaders learning to lead should focus on these critical leadership activities first and foremost.

As a leader learning to lead, here is a proven path to success:

> **Learn how to analyze employee performance and then provide what employees need to succeed.** Team members need clear expectations and ongoing feedback. They need resources and tools. They need skills and knowledge (training). They need meaningful consequences (positive and negative). They need help in setting and resetting priorities.

> **Learn how to communicate and connect with employees.** Everything is easier—more efficient and more effective—when employees trust their leaders and feel connected with them and the organization. Without this connection, some important things like coaching and engagement often just aren't possible.

> **Learn how to provide positive and constructive feedback.** Then do it—a lot. Feedback is to improving employee performance as a GPS is to reaching a desired location, continually reassuring when the employee is on the right path, while immediately but gently "recalculating" when the employee has veered off course.

> **Learn when to coach to take good performance to great (and build employee engagement) and when to have those difficult conversations to take unacceptable performance to acceptable.** They are very different conversations. Leaders need to learn the difference.

> **Learn how to coach effectively.** In a business environment, telling isn't coaching. Leaders need to use questions to encourage employee self-assessment; this builds a critical skill in the employee, but also helps develop a culture of continuous improvement.

Those responsible for developing leaders have an additional challenge: not only must your leadership development program include these skills (and others as necessary for your organization), but it must also present these skills in a way that is relevant, simple, easy to adopt, and immediately applicable to the job. Moreover, because leadership development doesn't only happen in a classroom, opportunities for practice and feedback on the job must be built in.

Learning and developing these competencies will put new leaders squarely on the road to effective leadership. But new leaders still must apply them—and reflect on them—day in and day out to shift their perspective of what's now important and to hone their craft. Which brings us to our next lie.

Lie #2: Damned Lie—I Don't Need Leadership Development

"I already know how to lead." "I went through leadership training X years ago (or at my previous job); why do I need to go again?" "I must be doing a good job because no one's told me otherwise." All are variations of the same concept—or lie—that leaders don't need leadership development.

One irony of leadership is that when workers are thrust into a leadership position, their ability to assess their own effectiveness declines dramatically. While they may be able to measure their team's sales or evaluate projects completed on time and under budget, their ongoing success is based largely on how they got those results. They may have made their numbers, but did they burn up their team? Is the team demoralized or disengaged? Often we really don't know as leaders. Employees often don't want to jeopardize their jobs by pointing out their leader's shortcomings; the leader's leader sees the numbers and, as long as there is no smoke, assumes everything is fine. And often leaders don't want to know what complaints their people may have because they wouldn't know how to fix them.

Studies suggest that managers may have an overinflated perception of how they are performing. A recent article, "Leaders Behaving Badly," suggests that leaders aren't leading (Frasch 2013). Specifically, of the 1,279 employees surveyed:

> 49 percent say their leaders never or only sometimes ask for their ideas to help solve problems.

> 47 percent say their leaders never or only sometimes help them solve problems without simply doing it for them.

> ➤ 45 percent say their managers never or only sometimes give sufficient feedback on their performance.

Less than half of the surveyed employees feel as though they're being led. And my experience at Entelechy in conducting 360-degree leadership surveys as part of our leadership development programs backs up those statistics. Often, leaders are surprised by the disconnection between how they thought they were doing and how their employees thought they were doing. In many cases, the disconnection unnerves the leader, because the feedback may be scathing. But in other cases, the disconnection is pleasantly surprising—the leader is doing better than expected, based on employee responses. Unnerving or surprising, the fact that a disconnection exists at all is telling: Leaders simply don't know how they are doing.

Leigh Branham, in "The Seven Hidden Reasons Employees Leave," wrote: "The keys to keeping and engaging employees are no big mystery, yet so many managers just don't see it" (Branham 2005). He draws from extensive research of exit interviews to highlight seven hidden reasons that employees leave a company. One reason most employees (60 percent of those interviewed) leave is because they believe they did not receive enough coaching and feedback. In contrast, I'd guess that most of the managers of those employees would say that they coached and provided enough regular feedback.

Marshall Goldsmith often claims that there is one thing that effective leaders do that other leaders don't: They build mechanisms to assess how they are performing, whether it's 360-degree surveys or one-on-one discussions with employees to ask what they can do to help the employees be more effective in their role. And Goldsmith suggests that the truly brave—and most effective—leaders invite employees to help them improve what they are working on. Companies could save billions of dollars on leadership development, Goldsmith believes, if their leaders simply asked for input (he calls it "feedforward") on their performance.

So when leaders claim that "I must be leading well because nobody's said anything to the contrary," it's a damned lie. When developing your leadership development plan, be sure to build in opportunities for leaders to receive input and feedback on their performance. And then teach your leaders how to overcome those built-in blind spots using feedforward or a similar technique.

Leaders often also claim that "I just went to leadership training a couple years ago; why do I need to go again?" That's akin to "I went to the gym last month, so I'm good." Effective leadership is a process of continuous development that requires ongoing attention. One Entelechy client, a CFO, explained it this way: "I have to get recertified in accountancy every year and attend training as part of that recertification. Leading people is at least as important—and 2.4 times more difficult—as determining EBITDA." Something is wrong with this picture.

Even if you did take a leadership course years ago, we fall out of good habits. Think about your last diet. It probably started well. You may have even lost some weight. But like most dieters, you eventually started to slip. And then one day you're out of the routine entirely.

Leadership development is a lot like that. You go to training and learn some nifty techniques to diligently apply back on the job. You see some positive results, and all is good. Then projects start to back up, quarterly reports are due, and the stress mounts. You resort to old habits, doing what you've always done—and getting what you've always gotten. To turn leadership skills into leadership habits, you need support, and ongoing leadership development is your support.

For those in charge of leadership development, consider these suggestions to address the lie leaders tell when they say they don't need leadership development:

> ➤ **Complete an annual 360-degree survey as a tool to refocus attention on critical leadership skills.** Marshall Goldsmith claims that what separates great leaders from good leaders is that great leaders understand the effect their behaviors have on others and also know how to change those behaviors. A 360-degree survey is a great tool for identifying behaviors that may be weighing others down and hurting performance.

> **Ensure that leadership training is current.** Those in leadership development shouldn't rehash the same old stuff. They should make the training worthwhile and focus on today's leadership challenges in the organization. What is your organization's current business challenge? Is it working more efficiently? Is it engaging and retaining high-potential employees? Is it reducing waste and improving quality? Just as leaders need a refresher from time to time, so too do your leadership development programs and strategies.

> **Look beyond traditional event-based leadership development and make leadership development a process.** Launching a new product? Build in a leadership component on evaluating the sales strategy and high-value customer needs. Reorganizing departments? Build in a leadership component on facilitating change. Reporting quarterly earnings? Build in a leadership component on communicating the company's vision. Having a company picnic? Build in a leadership component on relaying employee recognition. Capitalize on any opportunity to engage leaders in learning. Any time is a good time to develop leaders.

Lie #3: Statistical Lie—I Subscribe to the [Pick a Leadership Guru or Commercial Product] Approach to Leadership

Don't you love it when leaders come back from the latest leadership seminar featuring the current leadership guru? Then for the next couple months, you have to suffer through the oddball terms and obscure techniques that your boss learned at leadership camp until things settle back to normal (not better, just normal).

The most alluring lie about learning to lead is that we're doing the right things to create better leaders. According to industry-watchers Bersin & Associates, U.S. businesses spent $13.6 billion on leadership development in 2012, a 14 percent increase from the previous year (O'Leonard and Loew 2012). That's a lot of money. So shouldn't it have a measurable, meaningful impact on employee retention, engagement, and performance and company achievement of goals? You would think. But employee polls continue to conflict with what you would expect from such an investment. And I think those of us who work in leadership development are partly to blame.

We often sabotage leadership development by overlooking context. Instead of determining what our leaders need, we identify the latest leadership book and invite the guru to talk to our leaders. In a *McKinsey Quarterly* article "Why Leadership Development Programs Fail," the authors explain, "Too many training initiatives we come across rest on the assumption that one size fits all and that the same group of skills or style of leadership is appropriate regardless of strategy, organizational culture, or CEO mandate" (Gurdjian, Halbeisen, and Lane 2014).

Successful leadership development programs use consistent language throughout and have simple, yet effective, models. This is to avoid creating "Frankenleaders," a term coined by writer (and leadership guru himself) Marcus Buckingham. His article, "The Frankenleader Fad," describes the Frankenleader as the monster that's created when disjointed—and often conflicting—approaches, techniques, and theories are used during leadership development (Buckingham 2005).

To be clear, I am not criticizing gurus and their books—many are amazing (and my company has created training for 60 of them, including Warren Bennis, Jack Welch, Marshall Goldsmith, and Mike Abrashoff). Each guru carves out a unique and compelling facet of leadership, and each has his place, given the right organization facing the right challenges at the right time. But none alone provides the broad-based foundation of critical leadership skills required in a successful leadership development program.

We also overlook context by relying too heavily on commercial leadership development products. Jay Conger and Douglas Ready, in their paper *Why Leadership Development Efforts Fail*, cite what they call the "productization of leadership development" as a leading cause of leadership development failure (Conger and Ready 2003). Searching for quick fixes, we often rely on commercial leadership development products with limited relevance to our needs. We focus more on just using the products than on solving our problems. For a leadership development program to have a lasting, meaningful impact, the program needs relevance, simplicity, and—most of all—organizational alignment.

The whitepaper *Leadership Training That Sticks* offers 22 lessons from the past 21 years that can help organizations create lasting leadership change and sustained business impact (Traut 2014). While simple, the suggestions for successful leadership development require a concerted, orchestrated effort within the organization. Successful leadership development programs start at the top, with executive support and organizational alignment. Such programs must have buy-in and support at all levels of the organization; the message up and down the organization must be: "This is the way we lead." While an organization's products are known by their brand, the organization itself is known by its leadership and culture: People are attracted to organizations with strong leadership, and it's why they stay and engage.

Successful leadership development programs focus on challenges the organization faces and the explicit goals it wants to reach. Leadership development is about helping the organization grow through its people.

The lie that those in charge of leadership development are doing it right by consulting only leadership experts and commercial products is convincing because a lot of time and money is being invested in them. These experts and programs deliver training—sometimes really slick training—and their mantras are fairly easy to implement and even easier to sell. After all, what leader doesn't want to sit at the feet of a guru? Or participate in a multimodal, technology-infused whiz-bang leadership flight simulator? But it's important to remember that these gurus and products are not always the right thing for leaders in all organizations.

Conclusion

I haven't addressed all the fibs, white lies, half-truths, and errors of omission about learning to lead here, but I have discussed the three big ones and provided suggestions for dealing with them.

Learning to lead is easy. While leading at its core is fairly simple, changing our engrained (and often misguided) behaviors and beliefs—ones that have undeniably worked to our advantage for years—is not easy. To address this lie—that learning to lead is in fact easy—those responsible for developing leaders should outline the expected behavior at each leadership level; expectations of frontline leaders differ from those of midlevel leaders. They should train leaders on how to shift their perspectives on what's important in their new roles. They should link training directly to expectations by using scenarios that leaders face regularly at their companies. They should use simple, adaptable, and practical models in the training because leaders don't have enough time to break down more complex, theoretical models. And they should provide structured on-the-job support to ensure that models and techniques are, in fact, used—and continue to be used—on the job.

I don't need leadership development. Leadership positions often come with blindness. Fewer people want to, or are able to, provide meaningful feedback on how leaders are performing as they climb the leadership ladder. To address this lie—that leaders don't need additional leadership development—those responsible for developing leaders should implement some feedback processes, such as 360-degree (or 180-degree) assessments, to provide leaders with the input they need to succeed. Or if leaders aren't ready for such a direct form of input, those responsible for developing them should consider an organization-wide survey that provides more general input on leadership effectiveness. They should use the feedback to focus training on current challenges as part of the core leadership development program. And they should teach leaders how to ask for input in a way that demonstrates openness to continuous improvement.

I subscribe to the [pick a leadership guru or commercial product] approach to leadership. Basing a leadership development strategy on a leadership guru or a commercial product can create Frankenleaders out of disjointed and competing approaches, techniques, and theories. To address this lie—that the teachings of leadership gurus and their products should be implemented blindly—those responsible for developing leaders should seek out (if internal development is not an option) a tried and tested leadership development program that can be modified to fit the organization's culture and focus on organizational challenges. If purchasing a commercial product is the only option, they should make sure that it can grow and evolve as the organization changes and as the leadership focus evolves. And they should be judicious and deliberate in augmenting leadership development with books and presentations by leadership gurus. Instead of simply subscribing to the leadership guru of the day, they should make sure that the guru's theories don't conflict with the leadership development foundation already in place.

Training is one of the most rewarding industries. And training leaders is especially rewarding, because it cascades down the organizational chain: Well-developed, effective leaders have more confidence and success and thus their employees have more self-confidence, are more engaged with their work, and contribute more to their companies. Great employees join great companies led by great leaders. Their careers are more fulfilling when the organization abounds with great leaders—leaders who have learned to lead through great leadership development programs.

Having trained leaders at all levels since 1992, I understand the challenges of this important work. But take heart, organizational success—through leadership development—is truly in our hands.

References

Branham, L. 2005. "The Seven Hidden Reasons Employees Leave." Executive Update. The Center for Association Leadership, February. www.asaecenter.org/Resources/EUArticle.cfm?ItemNumber=11514.

Buckingham, M. 2005. "The Frankenleader Fad." *Fast Company*, September 1. www.fastcompany.com/54132/frankenleader-fad.

Charan, R., S. Drotter, and J. Noel. 2007. *The Leadership Pipeline: How to Build the Leadership Powered Company*. 2nd ed. San Francisco: Jossey-Bass.

Conger, J.A., and D.A. Ready. 2003. *Why Leadership Development Efforts Fail*. CEO Publication, May. Los Angeles: University of Southern California, Marshall School of Business, Center for Effective Organizations.

Frasch, K.B. 2013. "Leaders Behaving Badly." *Human Resource Executive Online*, October 31. www.hreonline.com/HRE/view/story.jhtml?id=534356316&.

Goldsmith, M., and M. Reitner. 2007. *What Got You Here Won't Get You There*. New York: Hyperion.

Gurdjian, P., T. Halbeisen, and K. Lane. 2014. "Why Leadership Development Programs Fail." *McKinsey Quarterly*, January. www.mckinsey.com/insights/leading_in_the_21st_century/why_leadership-development_programs_fail.

O'Leonard, K., and L. Loew. 2012. *Bersin & Associates Leadership Development Factbook*. Oakland, CA: Bersin & Associates.

Traut, T. 2014. *Leadership Training That Stinks*. Merrimack, NH: Entelechy.

6

Lies About Learning Strategies

Tina Busch

We all know the learning strategies, and leaders who implement them, that succeed and those that fail. There are plenty of good articles, books, and whitepapers with blueprints on how to build an effective learning strategy and how not to. And so with all the resources available, why do so many still get it wrong? Why are those who get it right able to replicate it across different companies and industries, under widely varying conditions?

First, let's step back and start with what learning strategy is and isn't. In this chapter, I use "learning strategy" not as instructional strategy or how we deliver or teach content, but rather as competitive strategy or how learning organizations make their companies more successful in the marketplace and how they operate as a strategic lever to achieve their desired business results. All businesses aim to achieve a competitive advantage—to acquire market share, accumulate customers, and win the war on talent. And no corporate organization does this without a learning strategy. Consider the questions required to win in business:

- ➤ What is the organizational vision?
- ➤ Who are our customers and markets?
- ➤ What goods and services do we provide?
- ➤ Who are the people and what is the culture we need to get us there?

➤ What technology, systems, or procedures are required to support the vision?

➤ How do we manage for the present and future win?

➤ What is our leadership style?

Businesses require the right people, and a successful learning strategy helps these people deliver and succeed based on the answers to the questions above.

Peter Drucker, referred to by *Businessweek* as "the man who invented management" once said, "The purpose of business is to create and keep a customer." If it were that simple, though, why doesn't every business win? Why doesn't every learning organization simply align to the business strategy and deliver? Why are learning professionals still talking about how to earn a seat at the table? In looking back over my career and talking to learning leaders about their experiences, there appears to be a pattern—a recipe for success or failure—and the recipe is not just for learning leaders, but also for leadership and business strategy in general. An organization's most vital competitive advantage is its people. It can have the best products, the best services, and the best infrastructure, but if it lacks the right people and learning strategies the organization will, eventually, lose its competitive advantage.

The strategies that fail almost always share a common trait. Despite looking good on paper and following best practice, they lack an understanding of and consideration for the complex aspects of any strategy: people and culture. They too often underestimate the importance of answering "Who are the people and what is the culture we need to get us where we want to be?"

Why does this happen, especially when we are in the people business? The answer is because we succumb to the lies we are told—and lies we tell ourselves—about what it takes to create a successful learning organization and to be a successful learning leader. And although I will suggest that we must, at times, forget about the softer or people side of strategy, it is those very people who will judge the effectiveness of our strategies and, possibly, the viability of our careers. In this chapter, I'll describe the five lies that I believe have the biggest impact on the development of effective learning strategies and offer approaches for avoiding them.

Lie #1: Data Are More Important Than Feelings

As learning leaders, we focus a lot on processes, frameworks, metrics, and data—for good reasons. They are fundamental to formulating strategies for how to run our business. But how often do we factor in our customer's feelings and the power of human behavior?

In 2010, Gap launched a new logo to refresh its image and appeal to a hipper, younger crowd. But the company lost sight of its target market—people who want the basics and aren't interested in trendy styles. Loyal customers felt disconnected from the new brand, and the logo failed to resonate with the new target audience. Gap's mistake was not in wanting to change and evolve, but in not being in touch with its customers' personas to ensure that the new brand strategy would connect. How does this happen?

You would expect that before implementing such a large change, Gap had analyzed data, held customer focus groups, and considered current and future trends. Lots of smart, hardworking people created and implemented this new logo, right? Perspectives on why "Gapgate" happened tended to focus on the logo itself—the font was too bland, the new image looked like child's clipart, and so on. But that wasn't the real problem. Despite having talented designers and marketers behind the launch, Gap debuted the new logo on its website without explaining the rebrand—without first understanding how its loyal customers felt about the original logo.

Much like the Gap logo debacle, learning leaders too often implement an agenda without first understanding the behavior, wants, and needs of their customers. We do this because while data may allow us to predict what a customer will purchase, no amount of quantitative data will tell us exactly why they do so. In formulating strategy, we need to not only understand the data but also take the time to determine what makes our customers tick. In other words, a successful learning strategy requires the learning leader to systematically study the people and culture in the organization. Otherwise known as ethnography, this method is used primarily by anthropologists. Thus a successful learning leader needs to be part businessperson (gathering data and using the models, frameworks, and processes in your arsenal) and part anthropologist (becoming immersed in the objective observation of the people and culture you seek to influence). And it's often what you learn as an anthropologist that drives a successful learning strategy—or one that fails.

So, how do you do this? In *The Moment of Clarity* (2014), Christian Madsbjerg and Mikkel Rasmussen outline a human science process called sensemaking, which simply and elegantly provides steps to observe our customers and their experiences in a business setting. The process follows five steps:

1. **Reframe the problem.** First, reframe a business problem in terms of the human experience or a phenomenon. To do so, shift the perspective from how the business sees the problem to how the customer sees it.

2. **Collect the data.** Thinking and acting like an anthropologist means collecting data in a way that might be very different from the norm. These data are not coming from surveys or scripted focus groups. Instead, engage in the lives of your customers with no preconceived notions or assumptions, while observing and collecting information. What might this look like? Sit with a business unit, region, or function for a few days. Or have lunch with your program participants.

3. **Look for patterns.** Once you have collected the data, look for patterns, connect the dots, and find any common themes.

4. **Create the key insights.** This is where the learning function can become a strategic lever for the business. Find the gaps

between the business assumptions and customers' experiences; that's where innovation occurs. What do the patterns tell you?

5. **Build the business impact.** Build value by translating your insights into initiatives within your strategy.

Sure, it's harder to quantify, but going through the ethnography process does more than create a new lens through which to think about and solve business problems. Unraveling the reasons behind customer decisions gives the customers a voice, and they will speak out loudly when their sensibilities are offended or, worse, not even considered. Gap experienced this firsthand within minutes of revealing the new logo on its website.

Lie #2: I Have Years of Education and Experience, I Know Best

Imagine that a foreign exchange student sits at the first meal with his new host family and tells them that what they eat and how they eat is all wrong. He then clears the table and resets it with the latest cutlery and cuisine from his country, the greatest in the world he tells them. The family is embarrassed by their struggle to use the new tools for eating the meal. The food, with its new smells, tastes, and textures, while interesting, causes considerable anxiety due to the vast differences. And the family is offended because the foreign student assumed their customs were wrong and undesirable.

Who would do that? Well, learning leaders do it every day. When we get a new assignment, we are like the foreign exchange student sitting with a host family—our customers. We often speak a different language, use our own tools and frameworks, and expect everyone to just go along because we said they should.

Having an ego and pushing an agenda without understanding or respecting the local culture will lead to failure every time. I once witnessed a learning leader join a global company and implement a one-size-fits-all strategy that was trendy at the time: Migrate all classroom learning to computer-based training. Knowing that the organization was in a cost-savings mode, he thought he could gain a quick win by moving to what seemed to be a more cost-effective learning model. However, what might have worked at a startup company in the high-tech industry with a younger employee base was not the right strategy for a century-old manufacturing organization comprising mostly baby boomers dispersed over 60 countries. He was quickly judged as being neither customer-centric nor inclusive. His customers thought that they had no voice and were being force-fed something they didn't understand or care to consume. So he was gone within a year, simply because he applied a strategy that seemed to make sense on paper and for the balance sheet, but didn't consider the organization's people and culture.

Despite years of experience and education, learning leaders often fail because they assume they know best. Showing arrogance, lacking stakeholder analysis, and not devoting enough energy to building social capital (the quantity and quality of relationships) and emotional capital (the ability to understand and leverage human behavior) will doom many a strategy. Showing respect and consideration for an organization's history and its people is critical to a successful learning strategy.

Lie #3: ADDIE Is Only for Instructional Design

Attention learning leaders—you already have the secret to creating good learning strategy in your arsenal: the ADDIE instructional design model, or any other instructional system design or performance improvement model for that matter. While some models may be considered more agile or less linear, they all have similar structures to analyze, design, and do it. Let's take a look, using ADDIE as a road map for learning strategy design (Figure 6-1).

Figure 6-1. The ADDIE Model

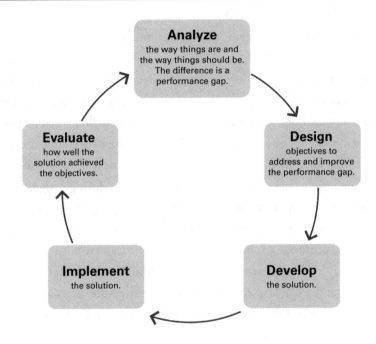

Analyze. Far too often, a learning strategy is designed, developed, implemented, and evaluated before a thorough current state analysis or needs assessment occurs. Analysis is not just about gathering the information to create a sound strategy. When done well, it allows you to build the network and relationships that will ensure stakeholder buy-in and successful implementation. During analysis, learning leaders should aim to thoroughly understand the way things happen today (the current state) and the preferred way (the desired or future state). Any differences represent opportunities for change or improvement (performance gaps).

Key questions for the analyze phase include:

➤ What are the current and future needs of the different business units, functions, and organization as a whole?

➤ What is the current state of learning?

➤ What works well and what needs change?

➤ Who is your audience?

➤ In what environment (culture, technology) does your audience operate?

Anyone familiar with instructional design knows that many more questions can be asked during analysis, and answering the ones above alone can be overwhelming, given the amount of data you might gather. Regardless, the next step is to synthesize. Very similar to the steps outlined in the sensemaking or ethnography process, you should next look for patterns and create insights, which will set you up for success during design.

Design. When designing the learning strategy, you should create objectives to address and, in the best possible world, eliminate performance gaps in the organization, building on what you learned during analysis. You should develop a learning philosophy, learning vision, and learning objectives, and judge how they will inform the structure, governance, and guiding principles for your learning strategy and the organization you create as a result.

Key questions for the design phase include:

➤ What are we trying to accomplish with a learning strategy?

➤ How does it align with the business strategy?

➤ What does it mean for individual contributors, managers, and senior leaders?

➤ How does it integrate with other key human resource and talent development initiatives?

➤ What does this vision suggest for the organization structure?

➤ Who are the learning and development staff and what work will they do?

➤ What kind of governance is required to meet the vision and objectives?

➤ What should be centralized or decentralized to better meet the needs of organization?

With the analysis and design complete, you have a blueprint for building a strategy that aligns with your customers' needs. It's time to develop.

Develop. When developing solutions, primary products and services, selection criteria, content delivery, outsourcing, and primary funding sources are the key elements of a learning strategy to consider.

Key questions for the develop phase include:

> ➤ What products and services are needed in the learning organization to support the business strategy?

> ➤ Who can use the learning products or services? Who receives what?

> ➤ What's mandatory versus recommended?

> ➤ How and where is training delivered?

> ➤ How does the way content is delivered differ for technical, compliance, soft skills, or other types of training?

> ➤ What aspects of learning are appropriate to outsource?

> ➤ How will we manage vendors?

> ➤ How are the services paid for?

> ➤ Who creates, makes decisions, and monitors the overall budget?

Implement. As the learning leader implements the solutions, there must be a strategy to promote, distribute, report, and maintain them.

Key questions for the implement phase include:

> ➤ Will implementation be enterprise-wide or local?

> ➤ What are the requirements for a common system?

> ➤ Who owns or tracks product and service use?

> ➤ How are programs promoted?

Evaluate. We've all heard the phrase "run training like a business." How we hold ourselves accountable for our results is a key indicator of the level of business orientation in the learning operation. Evaluation should include both operational and performance indicators so that efficiency and effectiveness are measured.

Key questions for the evaluate phase include:

➤ What are our success indicators?

➤ How is efficiency and effectiveness measured?

➤ Who owns or receives reports?

Consider conducting quarterly operational reviews with your primary stakeholders. Rarely will a learning leader be expected to conduct such a review, so you may have to ask for it. But this is not a bad thing, because it demonstrates to business leaders that you understand the role that learning plays in organizational success. During these reviews, share your metrics and ensure that you and the business leadership are aligned on what success looks like.

In this section, I intended to show how to use ADDIE to develop your learning strategy. This alone will not bring successful implementation. You'll also need to sell your strategy to the organization. See the next two lies for tips on positioning a learning strategy for acceptance by your customers.

Lie #4: Complex Organizations Require Complex Learning Strategies

Complex organizations don't require complex learning strategies. Why? Well, strategies must be embraced by stakeholders, and complex doesn't always mean better. For a learning organization to succeed, it must position itself as a strategic partner that helps deliver on the company's goals. In other words, run training as the business it is.

I like to express a learning strategy in the framework of a simplistic business model: producing products and services with a means (infrastructure) to transfer or sell it to your customers. The currencies we operate with are human and political capital—unless you happen to have a P&L for learning, which some organizations do. Using the term *sell* might sound like we're in a transactional business, and while there will always be an element of transactions in most businesses, learning organizations need to evolve from being transaction oriented to solution oriented. We are, after all, in the business of selling solutions.

Figure 6-2 is a three-tiered learning strategy, which, like most simple business models, has a portfolio of products and services that are deployed and managed through an infrastructure—think operations and supply chain. At the center are the customers or consumers. What follows is a case study that illustrates how this model has been deployed successfully.

Figure 6-2. Learning Strategy Model

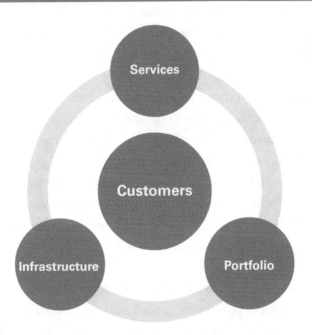

In 2010, a global consumer packaged goods company completed a human resource transformation, which included learning and development. In the past, learning and development in the company was global in name only. The department served primarily North America and was not scalable. The team performed mainly transactional work. The portfolio was not aligned to the business, and awareness and credibility were low. It was time for a change. The department performed a needs assessment, reviewing employee engagement surveys and conducting interviews with customers and stakeholders. The strategy used to transform learning and development followed the three tiers in Figure 6-2: services, portfolio, and infrastructure.

Services. The learning and development team had a credibility issue and perceived value was low. Awareness and use was mainly in North America, focused on transactional work such as program management and facilitation. Transactions (such as learning events) occurred, but solutions to business problems weren't provided. While a few programs generated positive reviews, none of the business leaders believed the learning organization was a strategic lever for business results.

Needing to demonstrate strategic value, the team created a new role—performance consultant. Consultants capable of working within the highly complex organization and implementing solutions that could improve individual and team performance were aligned to each of the company's business units and functional groups. Responsible for partnering with business and human resource leaders, conducting needs assessments, and identifying and implementing performance improvement solutions, these consultants made up a newly formed services division in the learning organization.

Portfolio. The existing portfolio of learning products was not aligned to the business and served only a small segment of the company's U.S. population. Needing to stretch the budget to reach more employees with relevant content, portfolio managers worked with the performance consultants to identify the common skills gaps. Partnering with procurement, the portfolio managers sourced content providers who could support a global population in the prioritized areas. And creating several strategic vendor partnerships, the company had its first fully aligned global portfolio of learning content.

Infrastructure. The company then needed the technical infrastructure to help manage the portfolio and market its products and services. The current learning management system was outdated, available to North America only, and used only partly by the organization to which it was available. A global learning council of learning and talent representatives from all regions, businesses, and functions was formed to identify what the new learning management system would need to support the organization's diverse needs.

After implementation, the new system gained immediate buy-in from the learning and talent representatives because they were part of the decision-making process. Involving the learning and talent representatives was critical because they were the ones who decided if, and how, the new system would be used, and they were the champions of the system to customers. In other words, regardless of their level in the organization, these representatives were key decision makers and change agents.

Customers. Customers are the center of the learning strategy. The services, portfolio, and infrastructure were all developed with the customers' needs in mind.

Your strategy is your vision. The learning strategy this company used was simple in structure, although it was executed in a highly complex environment. In the end, a simple strategy is easier to sell, both to customers and stakeholders.

Lie #5: I'm a Learning Professional, Not a Salesperson

Leadership is all about selling, and the best learning professionals are selling every day. They are highly skilled in many of the same competencies required to be a great salesperson, such as communicating a vision, building and maintaining relationships, inspiring confidence, influencing and persuading, and managing change. Let's take a closer look at these competencies and how they might apply to learning.

Communicating a vision and goals. You may think you are selling the products, services, and infrastructure that make up the strategy, but you're actually communicating the vision of what the strategy will do for the organization and how it will make people feel. To do so effectively, learning leaders must excel at verbal and written communication and exude an executive presence.

Building and maintaining relationships. Ensuring that the product or service aligns with the customers' needs and thus resonates with them can help you build and maintain professional customer relationships. When decision making takes a customer-oriented perspective, the work will be easier and far more rewarding.

Inspiring confidence. Since we can't make our customers simply accept our vision and strategy, we have to inspire in them confidence to do so.

Influencing and persuading. Your ability to connect with people emotionally and convince them of the value and appropriateness of your vision and strategy is what will ultimately drive success.

Managing change. If no one buys, nothing changes. If no one follows, leadership is lacking. Learning professionals are in the change business, and selling change requires great relationship management, influence, and persuasion. Learning professionals are salespeople, and, more specifically, great learning professionals are great salespeople.

Figure 6-3 illustrates a simple sales process. You will recognize several of the ADDIE elements in it, but it also includes some stakeholder management steps, such as establishing the relationships, presenting the solution, and negotiating or closing the sale.

Figure 6-3. Sales Process Model

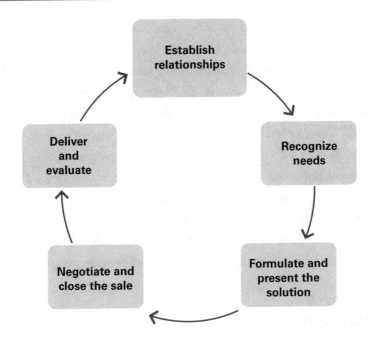

One selling skill to remember is to not put the sale first. If your stake-holders or customers suspect you are putting the sale before their interests (or driving your own agenda), the relationship suffers, and you won't make the sale anyway.

Conclusion

In this chapter, we explored five lies that separate the good learning strategies from the bad. A common theme is that they all have people and culture interdependencies. Lies #1 (data are more important than feelings) and #2 (I have years of education and experience, I know best) provided tips to success in designing learning strategies: Consider the what (data) and why (feelings) in your analysis; respect and consider the organization's history and culture. Your experience and education loses value if you can't connect with your customers.

Lie #3 (ADDIE is only for instructional design) recommends using ADDIE, a familiar tool, in designing the learning strategy. With people and culture components embedded throughout the model, it can help you break down the design process. Lie #4 (complex organizations require complex learning strategies) is also about design, and the reminder to keep it simple. Complex strategies are hard to sell and often unnecessary.

And finally Lie #5 (I'm a learning professional, not a salesperson) may be the most important and most difficult. A design is only as good as its ability to get sold, and that takes strong leadership.

At the center of each of these lies is the customer—the secret to success. Learning leaders who keep their customers close in mind while developing strategies from analysis through implementation increase their chances of success.

Reference

Madsbjerg, C., and M. Rasmussen. 2014. *The Moment of Clarity*. Boston: Harvard Business Review Press.

Recommended Reading

Carnegie, D. 1981. *How to Win Friends and Influence People*. Rev. ed. New York: Simon and Schuster.

Conrad, D. 2011. "Great Leaders Are Great Salespeople." *Strategic Leadership Review* 1(2): 9–15.

Dick, W., and L. Carey. 1996. *The Systematic Design of Instruction*. 4th ed. New York: Harper Collins College Publishers.

Eikenberry, K. 2010. "Five Reasons Why Every Leader Is a Salesperson." Leadership & Learning (blog), August 23. http://blog.kevineikenberry .com/leadership/five-reasons-why-every-leader-is-a-salesperson.

Lies About the Return on Learning

David Vance

Return on learning is a topic many people have strongly held beliefs about and aren't afraid to share them. I was once asked to join a group of my colleagues for a two-hour discussion on the return on investment (ROI) for learning. I was happy to oblige and looked forward to a good discussion on its application in our field. When the moderator asked how many of us used ROI, I was the only one—of the 15 people in the room—who said yes. The group proceeded to catalog the reasons why ROI should never be used. So it turns out I was invited to be the token ROI supporter, which was fine because I believe ROI can play an important role in learning. But I learned that day how truly controversial this topic is in the learning field.

Why all the fuss? And why the passionate debate? Well, I think there are many misunderstandings about ROI for learning. In this chapter, I will try to sort them out by examining eight lies on the topic. I will then provide a framework for confronting—and dealing with—these lies, which I hope will allow practitioners to benefit from key insights, while avoiding the common pitfalls.

But first, here's a little background on ROI for learning. Jack Phillips introduced the concept in his 1983 book, *Handbook of Training*

Evaluation and Measurement Methods. It is often referred to as Level 5 of learning evaluation, supplementing the four levels introduced by Don Kirkpatrick in 1959. Recall that Level 4 in the Kirkpatrick framework is results, which Phillips refers to as impact. Phillips starts with impact and then assigns it a dollar value, which becomes the gross benefit or bottom-line impact of the learning before learning costs are considered. The next step is to subtract the total cost of the learning (accounting costs like development and delivery, plus the opportunity cost or value of the participant's time) to determine the net benefit to the organization from investing in the learning program. Finally, ROI can be calculated as the net benefit divided by total cost and expressed as a percentage.

Return on Learning Example

Suppose the impact (Level 4 of the Kirkpatrick framework) of a training initiative is a 2 percent increase in sales, of which the sales or accounting department determines the bottom-line impact is $500,000. The learning and development department calculates the total cost of the training to be $300,000. We can now calculate the net benefit and the ROI of the training:

> **Net benefit: Gross benefit ($500,000) – Total cost ($300,000) = $200,000**
>
> **ROI: Net benefit ($200,000) / Total cost ($500,000) = 40 percent**

Both the net benefit and ROI compare benefits with costs, with the net benefit as a unit of money and ROI as a percentage.

These equations allow us to create a traditional business case for learning, in which the benefits of an investment are explicitly compared with the costs, providing the information a decision maker needs to decide whether to fund a project and to determine whether it was a good investment. The case can be made by looking at just the net benefit ($200,000) or the ROI (40 percent) of the learning project.

In this chapter, I use the term *return on learning* to include any use of net benefit, ROI, or similar measure to compare the benefit of a training program with the cost. We will start by examining five lies that support not calculating a return on learning, and then continue by examining four lies about using ROI in particular.

Lie #1: We Don't Need to Measure Return on Learning

The most common lie I hear for not calculating a return on learning is simply "We don't need to measure it." In short, the argument is that leaders know we are doing a good job and thus no one is asking to see a return. Let's explore this in three parts.

We are actually doing good work, and our leaders believe they are getting a good return on their investment.

While I appreciate the trust senior leaders place in my learning colleagues and the outstanding relationships many have with their CEOs, we have an obligation to make a business case for large investments and to determine how those investments have performed. Note that I'm not suggesting we compute a return on learning for every program. Doing so consumes valuable time and resources. But we should for all large programs—in budget or number of participants. To not is simply an abrogation of our fiduciary responsibility as managers.

There are two good reasons to calculate the return on learning. First, you will learn more about your program's costs and benefits by analyzing them, which will allow you to improve the program, if necessary. When I was the chief learning officer of Caterpillar University, we projected a return on learning for our major programs and conducted three post-deployment return-on-learning studies every year. These studies helped us continually improve. Second, your supportive CEO may not always be there, or your organization's financial picture may change. The best leaders are always prepared and do not take funding for granted.

We are actually not doing good work.

Learning leaders may think that their return is high on all large programs, but they won't know for sure if they don't calculate a return on learning. Many learning leaders mistakenly assume that their programs offer significant value when, in fact, they do not. And even if their program quality is high and the impact significant, they still do not know if the benefits outweigh the costs without doing the analysis. Would your organization's leaders consider it good work if the costs exceeded the expected benefits? How would you identify opportunities to increase the impact or achieve the same impact but at lower cost without calculating a return on learning?

Your leaders are not convinced.

For his 2010 book *Measuring for Success*, Jack Phillips surveyed 96 CEOs on what information about learning was most important to them. First was alignment of learning to their top goals, and second was ROI. So no matter what many learning leaders think, the fact is that their CEOs want to see the business case for the learning organization and for high-budget programs. CEOs expect the same from all other departments and for all major investments; this is simply how business is conducted. But in many organizations, learning professionals have not been asked to follow this disciplined planning process, damaging their credibility and explaining why many learning leaders are lacking in influence. Quite simply, they have not earned it.

So in the end, even if you think your leaders believe you are adding value, you should measure the return on learning (either the net benefit or ROI) for your largest and most discretionary programs. This will ensure that you are delivering the promised value and are in a position to continually improve.

Lie #2: Return on Learning Cannot Be Calculated

The second most common lie I hear for not calculating a return on learning is that it cannot be calculated. Many learning leaders would like to calculate the return on learning, but they say that it isn't possible and thus isn't worth pursuing further.

Return on learning most certainly can be calculated. Jack and Patti Phillips and others have written numerous books explaining in great detail how to do so. Calculating a program's net benefit or ROI requires just three measures: the program's impact, the monetary value of that impact, and the program's cost. These three measures can be forecast or estimated. At this point, some leaders will say that forecasts and estimates are subjective and unreliable—and thus inaccurate—and that the impact of the training program cannot be isolated from other factors contributing to reaching the goal (like a 10 percent increase in sales). Let's look closer at these two objections.

Accuracy

It is true that calculating a return on learning requires forecasting (before the program is developed and deployed) or estimating (after the program is deployed or completed). Organizations frequently forecast outcomes before actual data are in hand to learn more about what is possible and achievable in the future, not to predict with 100 percent accuracy. Learning leaders should adopt the same practice. Claiming that the forecasts of a return on learning will not be accurate is not a valid reason for not calculating them. Learning leaders must make the best forecasts possible, based on their experience with similar programs, their knowledge of the value learning investments will create in the coming year, and inputs from their customers or anyone else who can provide useful information.

After a program has been delivered and the costs are known, organizations still must estimate the impact of the program to calculate the return. Even here, they don't need 100 percent accuracy to gain value from the exercise. They want to know if the actual return was close to the forecast return. Perhaps the forecast was too optimistic or too pessimistic. Or perhaps the forecast was fine but the plan wasn't executed properly, resulting in a weaker impact or higher costs. Organizations look to use this information to better deliver the planned results the next time around. They want to learn from the difference between what they thought would happen and what actually happened. Learning leaders need to take a similar approach—make forecasts, monitor variances, replan, and then repeat, becoming more accurate over time.

Isolation of Learning

Not being able to isolate the impact of learning from other factors is one of my favorite reasons learning leaders use for not attempting to calculate a return on learning. Proponents of this reason may admit that costs could be calculated and may even admit that a dollar value could be assigned to impact if we could only isolate the impact of learning. Let's take a common learning example to explore this objection. Say the company has a goal to increase sales by 10 percent next year and the senior vice president of sales agrees that training, if properly designed, delivered, and reinforced, could contribute to reaching that goal. (The training may, for example, consist of a course on consultative selling skills and a course on product features.) Now the question is how much this training could achieve, by itself in isolation from all the other factors.

In this example, we may expect that an improving economy would play a large role in higher sales. The company may be introducing new products with better features that should lead to higher sales. And, perhaps, the company may also have implemented a sales incentive system and hired five new salespeople. All these factors will play a role in generating higher sales. So how much sales growth can we attribute solely to training? This example illustrates the isolation issue, which, for many, is an insurmountable obstacle to calculating the return on learning. It needn't be.

First, let's be clear about our standards. We are not looking for perfection or absolute certainty, which does not exist in the real world of business. Your CEO, board of directors, and senior leaders know this. But some HR colleagues do not. They worry about sharing a forecast or estimate with senior leaders and then being asked to "prove it." Unfortunately, there is no "prove it" when it comes to a business plan or forecast about the future, because the future has not yet happened. So in most circumstances, your leaders will not ask you to prove it. Now, if we are talking about calculating a return on learning for a completed project, they may ask us to prove it. So, as we will discuss at the end of the chapter, we want to be smart about how we present our results. In either case, our standard is to be roughly right or close enough to make the right business decision (proceed with the program or not) if done proactively, or to draw the right conclusions from the return on learning study if done after the fact. We don't have to be exactly right, and we are not publishing these results in a scholarly journal. We are in the business world trying to make the best decisions we can with limited information in an environment of unrelenting uncertainty. As a result, "good enough for business" is our standard.

Now that we are on the same page with regard to our standards, let's see how the isolation issue can be addressed. For planning purposes, the best way is to engage the sponsor—the senior vice president of sales in our example. If you have any pertinent historical information available (like from previous after-the-fact studies for similar programs) share it. If not, discuss all the possible factors that might contribute to an increase in sales. Ask questions. For example, how important is the learning initiative relative to the other factors? Is it the single most important factor (usually not) or is it one of several important factors that might influence results? Is it important but not as important as one or two others? You might ask the sponsor to prioritize all the factors on the list. This exercise alone will give all involved a pretty good idea of the relative importance of the training program. Because all of the factors together will contribute 100 percent toward reaching the goal, asking about the relative importance of each factor can provide additional important information.

So if the goal is to increase sales by 10 percent and there are five important factors, with learning in the middle, you, with the help of your key stakeholders, might assign a factor of 20 percent to the training program. In other words, the isolated expected impact of learning is a 2 percent (10 percent x 20 percent) increase in sales. Then, you must find someone in sales or accounting to help calculate the bottom-line impact of a 2 percent increase in sales, which is the amount that can be directly attributed to training.

This sounds very subjective. Well, of course it is. All forecasts and business plans are. They represent an organization's educated guess (forecast) about events that have not yet occurred. They are based on historical data and the economic environment, but they are, in the end, guesses. In the end, the point is that we followed a process and engaged the right people to create the best forecast we could, based on the information available. That is all a management team can expect. I did this at Caterpillar for five years and for two different CEOs, and I was never asked to reduce my net benefit forecasts. In fact, by the end, I was told that my forecasts were too conservative.

Finally, let's look at the isolation issue when calculating the return on learning after the completion of a program. In this case, the industry standard methodology is to ask a random sample of participants to estimate the percentage impact on their results that can be attributed solely to the training program. They are then asked to rate their level of confidence in the estimate they just provided. The two percentages, multiplied together, result in the "confidence-adjusted isolation factor" for that individual. An average is taken over the sample to determine the confidence-adjusted isolation factor for the program. This is, of course, self-reported data, but an adjustment has been made allowing for some subjectivity. (Note that there are other methods to isolate impact, like using a control group, but this is the easiest and can always be done. See Phillips [1983] for all the potential methods.)

It is important to remember why we are doing this and what our standard is. We want to see if the program's results are close to what we expected (our forecast), see what we can learn and how we can improve the program, and build a library of actual results to help us forecast future results accurately.

Lie #3: We Won't Learn Anything

There is a backward logic that learning leaders use when claiming that they won't learn anything from an ROI. They should calculate an ROI, and then determine if they learned anything. Not the other way around. So unless learning leaders believe they already know everything worth knowing, there is an opportunity to learn and improve by evaluating the return on learning. Whether the exercise turns out to be worthwhile will depend on what is learned and at what cost. But that can only be determined after the fact.

In my experience at Caterpillar, asking staff to think about the return on learning—the expected application rate for the learning, the performance support and sponsor engagement required to produce the desired application rate, the expected impact, the monetary value of that impact, and the accounting and opportunity costs for the program—always produced valuable insights and led to changes in how we planned to design, deploy, and reinforce the learning. Put simply, our programs would not have had the same effect on our company's results had we not subjected ourselves to the business discipline of exploring the expected return on our learning investments. But keep in mind that the level of effort in calculating the return on learning must be proportionate to the budget for the program. We reserved this effort for our larger programs.

Lie #4: Calculating a Return on Learning Costs Too Much and Takes Too Long

The method described under Lie #2 of reaching an agreement with stakeholders on the isolated impact of learning can be completed in one to two hours. Assigning a monetary value to that impact may take one to two hours, and calculating the costs of the proposed program may take another several hours. Altogether, calculating a return on learning could be completed in fewer than 10 hours and with no outside assistance. And given that the process is reserved for large programs, the investment is small, especially when compared with the amount being invested in designing, developing, and delivering the learning solution.

Calculating a return on learning after a program is complete could take more or less time, depending on the sample size and the method used to solicit the self-reported estimate of impact. Some organizations automate this process and send surveys to participants three to six months after a program in order to obtain the confidence-adjusted isolation factor, which can then be used to estimate impact. Total time involved in these calculations should be less than 10 hours. Or if conducting a 15–30 minute telephone interview with each participant, it would probably take 20 to 30 hours for a sample size of 30 participants, given the logistics involved. This should be manageable for a limited number of post-program return-on-learning studies.

Another option is to hire an expert in the discipline, which may give the results increased credibility, if funding is available. The consultant could cost $10,000 to $25,000 per study, which may be prohibitive in some situations.

Regardless of the preferred method, the cost of estimating and measuring the impact of a learning solution for a major initiative will most likely be dwarfed by the cost of the solution itself.

Lie #5: No One Will Believe the Return on Learning

Unfortunately, the lie that no one will believe the return on learning becomes a truth more often that it should. If we manage our training function like a business and convey our results with humility (meaning that we acknowledge the role of forecasts and estimates), we are likely to have credibility. But even if we don't overstate or misuse the results, our stakeholders may still not believe us—and they shouldn't.

Here is the issue. After Jack Phillips introduced the concept of ROI for learning in 1983, many learning leaders latched onto ROI as a way to demonstrate their worth, validate their existence, and protect their budgets when senior leaders started to question the return on their learning investments. But a good ROI is not always enough to assuage the concerns of senior leaders.

Senior leaders start to show concern when learning leaders appear to not be managing the company's assets and investments the same way that other business leaders do. When senior leaders don't see basic management principles being applied, they naturally start to wonder whether they are getting value for their investment in learning. So they start to ask questions about how much is being spent, what it is being spent on, and what tangible business results they are getting for their investment. In this environment, ROI would seem like a perfect way to show the value of learning. If learning leaders could just show high ROI, the questions would stop, right?

Well, most senior leaders are smarter than that. Why would they be impressed with a high ROI for a program that is not aligned to the organization's goals? Why would they believe a high ROI forecast when there was no input from stakeholders on how the ROI should be assessed? And wouldn't they be naturally suspicious of a high ROI number that surfaced just a month after they started questioning the spending on a particular program or suggesting that the learning budget be cut? So when the function is not being run like a business, when the learning leader has little credibility with senior leaders, and when a high ROI appears out of nowhere to defend a program under question, it is easy to understand why senior leaders might be suspicious.

But it does not have to be this way. Learning leaders can run their departments like a business, implement a governance model, maintain close relationships with senior leaders, and integrate return on learning into their regular planning and audit processes with transparency and accountability. This means telling senior leaders and governing boards what the expected return on learning should be for key programs, keeping them up to date on interim results, and sharing the actual results—good and bad—when projects are completed.

Most of all, learning leaders need to reinforce why they calculate and share the return on learning—to encourage better planning, enable better execution, and generate the information needed to continually improve. It is to ensure that investments in learning produce the best possible return for the organization, not to justify programs or defend department budgets under fire.

Lie #6: We Should Prioritize Programs With High Returns on Learning

Some learning leaders who regularly forecast returns on learning for their key programs fall into the trap of trolling for the highest return. They prioritize programs by expected ROI and use this to decide which programs to fund. This is both a mistake and an improper use of ROI.

Return on learning should not take the place of strategically aligning learning to the organization's highest priority goals. Alignment should start with a discussion with critical stakeholders about next year's goals, along with their relative priority. The learning leaders should work with stakeholders to determine how learning can contribute to reaching these goals and what the expected isolated impact will be. At this point, the learning leaders will know the organization's key priorities to which they can align training investment.

Imagine a table showing the organization's goals in order of priority and under each goal is the name of one or more training programs that will help reach it, along with the expected impact, the cost of the program, the net benefit, and the ROI. The estimated training investment would be allocated according to organizational priorities until the funds ran out.

Now imagine a learning-centric table that lists training programs by ROI, ignoring the goal the programs support. It may be that the programs with the highest ROI support the lowest priority goal. Which programs would stakeholders fund first: the ones with an acceptable ROI that support high-priority goals, or ones with a high ROI that support lower priority goals? This is a no-brainer.

As long as the programs have an acceptable ROI, stakeholders will choose to fund them in the order of the goals they support. This approach will maximize the impact the learning investment will have on the organization's results, although it may not maximize the ROI of the learning investment. As long as the mission of the learning function is to support reaching the organization's goals, this is the approach to take.

Note that ROI can be used to rank programs for funding when multiple programs support the same goal. For example, if three programs supported a low-priority goal, but there was not enough budget to fund all three, the program with the highest ROI should be funded first, followed by the program with the next highest ROI.

Lie #7: Return on Learning Is the Only Way to Demonstrate Value

While return on learning is the most powerful method to demonstrate value, it is a lie to suggest that it is the only way to demonstrate value. Application (Level 3 of the Kirkpatrick framework) and impact (Level 4) also demonstrate value. After all, if you did a thorough needs analysis and identified that applying a new skill was required to improve performance, it is logical to conclude that the successful application of that skill demonstrates value. Likewise, a training program that results in a 2 percent increase in sales unquestionably has value.

But if we stop there, how do we know if the project is worth doing? Senior leaders always want to improve performance, but only if it makes sense to do so. No one would suggest spending $100,000 for a one-time performance improvement valued at $25,000. Return on learning only helps provide decision makers with what they need to make an informed investment decision—a comparison of benefits (value) and costs.

Lie #8: ROIs for Learning and Finance Are Calculated the Same Way

Some people assume that ROI for learning is the same as ROI for other financial investments. While both are designed to determine whether a project is worth pursuing, the numerator and the denominator in the equation are different. In finance and accounting, the numerator would most often be the current value of a multiyear stream of net benefits, and the denominator would be the value of the investment required to produce the stream of benefits. The investment would be a balance sheet asset item, such as the capital cost of a new piece of equipment.

In contrast, the equation for an ROI for learning typically consists of a numerator that represents the net benefit for just one year (although it could be the current value of multiple years), with the net benefit calculated as the net financial benefit less the opportunity cost of the participants' time. The denominator for a learning ROI is cost, comprising expense items from the income statement (not the balance sheet), such as salaries and consultant fees, and the opportunity cost, which doesn't appear in any financial statement.

So if your accountants tell you that your ROI for a training program is not a true ROI (in a financial sense), they are right. A learning ROI is not strictly a financial ROI, but rather a convenient tool to help us compare costs and benefits in order to decide whether a program is worth developing (or how much value the program actually delivered, if calculated after its completion). If calling this calculation an ROI causes push back from the financial branch of your organization, just change the name. You might call it return on learning (ROL), which is what we did at Caterpillar when our accountants objected to our use of the term *ROI*. Once we labeled it something other than ROI, they were fine.

Conclusion

I hope you now have a better feel for the return on learning concept and the lies or misconceptions surrounding its use. Without a doubt, some learning leaders misuse return on learning. They dismiss it outright because they believe (mistakenly) that it can't be calculated or that they won't learn anything from it. They claim that it costs too much or takes too long to calculate. They assume that their senior leaders will not believe the return on learning. They prioritize programs with high returns on learning, rather than ensuring that the programs align to their organization's goals. They think that calculating it is the only way to demonstrate value to senior leaders. And they assume that their learning ROI is identical to a financial ROI. But perhaps the most pervasive excuse is that learning leaders don't need to do it because they know how great they are and that their senior leaders are not asking for it.

Return on learning is a very powerful concept. It is the only way to make a business case for a large, expensive discretionary program. And it is an excellent tool to explore a program's actual impact in order to identify future opportunities for improvement. ROI and net benefit are simply numbers, inherently neither good nor bad. If someone misuses them the fault lies with the practitioner, not the concept or the calculation. So let's not dismiss the best way we have to compare costs and benefits. Instead, let's use it wisely to make better decisions, to learn, and to continually improve.

To avoid the pitfalls in using return on learning to make a business case, follow these steps:

1. Always start with your organization's goals. Know your stakeholders' goals and how they are prioritized.

2. Meet with the owner of each goal to understand if and how a learning program can help reach it. Or if someone else asks you to create a program, make sure that it aligns to a high-priority goal.

3. If it does, agree on the specifics of the program with stakeholders, including the expected cost and benefit. These will be forecasts, and subject to error, but that is okay. This is how organizations plan. It is an imperfect, messy process, but you will be more successful having gone through it.

4. Share your forecast and assumptions with other leaders and solicit their comments and feedback. Make appropriate changes. Be humble and transparent. Remember why you are doing this: You want to make the right decisions about key programs and you want to improve. And remember that your forecast should simply be close enough to inform the decision-making process.

Likewise, to avoid misusing return on learning after a pilot or project is complete, follow these steps:

1. Discuss the expected impact of the program with the stakeholders before starting the program. Agree on the expected isolated impact or a proxy for it to measure success.

2. Meet with stakeholders as the program is deployed to share interim results or leading indicators. Ask how they believe it is going and whether they are still comfortable with the expected impact.

3. Be conservative in estimating the isolated impact. Value it the same way you valued it in the business case before the program was started.

4. Present your results with humility and in the spirit of continual learning. If the results differ widely from what you had forecast, try to understand why, and view this as a learning opportunity. Present both the good and the bad. This will increase your credibility.

If you are new to the return on learning concept, there are many books and workshops on ROI to get you started. You should then look for a program to try it with and see what you learn. Then do it again. And again. Pretty soon you will be amazed by how much you have learned and how your skills to deliver value to your organization have improved.

References

Phillips, J.J. 1983. *Handbook of Training Evaluation and Measurement Methods*. Houston, TX: Gulf Publishing Division.

Phillips, J.J., and P.P. Phillips. 2009. *Measuring for Success*. Alexandria, VA: ASTD Press.

Recommended Reading

Phillips, P.P., and J.J. Phillips. 2006. *Return on Investment Basics*. Alexandria, VA: ASTD Press.

Part III

Lies About Technology and Learning

8

Lies About E-Learning

Michael W. Allen

Perhaps no segment of the learning field has more misconstrued principles that lead to ineffective practices than e-learning. To be fair, designing and developing effective e-learning can be difficult, so success is far from a sure thing. But there are plenty of popular lies that attempt to excuse unimpressive results and justify poor e-learning programs. There are more that suggest that lame attempts truly are enough. There are even more that try to assure the wary that new technologies make improving performance fast and easy.

Misunderstandings are so pervasive that some lies have corresponding counter-lies—lies at each extreme—from "it's too hard" to "nothing to it," from horrendously expensive to miraculously cheap, from scourge of the earth to savior of humanity. As with most things, we prefer the comfort of extreme judgment—black or white, good or bad. But the truth is often somewhere in the middle; it depends on specifics, not on generalizations.

One chapter is not enough to address all the lies about e-learning, so I'll take up the misconceptions that I hear most often—pointing perhaps to the less comfortable middle ground where the truth nestles and where we have to be thoughtful in drawing conclusions and making decisions. But note that despite what the lies imply, there are few absolute rights and wrongs. Countering the extremes of lies with more extremes simply exacerbates the problem and adds to the confusion.

Lie #1: Technology Makes Instruction Less Expensive

I often hear how alluring e-learning can be. How you can deliver it more easily than face-to-face instruction. How once you've automated instruction, you can take on any number of students and confidently know they'll all receive the same instruction. How after some careful preparation up front, you can sit back and let the computer do all the heavy lifting. How you can organize content for presentation, present it, and follow up with a final test, just as you can in the classroom. How once it's done, it's done.

But instructional design for automated delivery requires more, not less, work than instructor-led delivery. Why? Because no matter how smart the designer or how clever the design, the learning product lacks the instructor's real-time adjustments that greatly influence the quality and effectiveness of each delivery. While we may someday have artificial intelligence that can perform spontaneous instructional tasks and make subtle adjustment to the learning experience, for now programming must attempt to proactively address every possibility and account for every individual need. Only the instructional functions that are anticipated, designed, and built will be carried out.

E-learning is a great way to save money and reliably improve performance—a win/win. But it's important to save money at the right place, instead of in places where cutting costs guarantees little or no impact and wastes time and effort. E-learning dramatically reduces delivery costs, typically the largest instructional costs. With e-learning there are no travel expenses, no classroom requirements, no instructor costs, and no scheduling problems that may require an operational shutdown while people are being trained.

But don't get greedy. Apply some of the expected savings to improving the design and development of the courseware. Failing to do so may result in learning products with little impact, wasted development costs, untrained learners, and lost opportunity costs. And then, of course, the need for effective training remains.

The message here is simple—developing effective e-learning programs will cost more up front than developing classroom instruction for the same content. But done right, e-learning can provide highly individualized learning experiences that take advantage of every minute learners are away from their jobs for training. And while it may cost more to develop, in the end it may save money when factoring in the costs and limitations of traditional classroom training.

Lie #2: Instructional Design for E-Learning Is Too Hard

I also hear complaints that instructional design for e-learning is too difficult, too slow, and too expensive. Let's agree that good instructional design and development isn't easy—especially when doing it the traditional way many of us were taught: the ADDIE (analysis, design, development, implementation, and evaluation) way. For decades, practitioners have extolled the virtues of what began as a phase-sequenced process—analysis before design, design before development, and so forth (Branson et al. 1975)—and have exhaustively detailed the tasks required within each phase, insisting on the importance of thoroughness, lest the following phases be affected by errors in preceding phases. ADDIE is very logical, but if followed religiously, it can be too hard, too slow, and too expensive to implement, especially for e-learning.

For quite some time, ADDIE users have been searching for more practical methods—methods that don't make them feel guilty about breaking the rules. While it is true that all ADDIE's tasks are important, is there a way to complete them more quickly? How can the risk of errors and the potential damage caused by missing or skipping steps be mitigated so that tedious, painful, and expensive thoroughness isn't required?

One option is the Successive Approximation Model (SAM), which is a much better approach for many in our profession (Allen and Sites 2012). In what could be seen as the next step in ADDIE's evolution,

SAM incorporates rapid prototyping, agile software development, interleaving design, and development and iteration—all adapted for the needs of e-learning professionals as well as the needs of the production team and stakeholders.

SAM is a bit more of a "just do it" process. While ADDIE takes a long time to generate specification documents, which are often interpreted differently by their writers and the assortment of readers for whom they are intended, SAM requires only a quick survey of the situation, mostly to determine who knows what and who cares about what. Key players are then assembled to brainstorm what might be done. Under the leadership of a skilled instructional designer, the group is encouraged to imagine a solution and then address the question: Why shouldn't we do this? (The "this" is usually prototyped quickly so that everyone has a clear understanding of what's being proposed.) Addressing that question generates valuable, specific information quickly and expedites conducting analysis and designing creative solutions.

Overall, SAM is simpler, faster, more practical, more learner focused, and less content focused than other models. It recognizes the need for clients and subject matter experts to be informed and defines practical ways for them to participate in instructional development. It takes advantage of the contributions learners can make from the very start of the process. It works to identify key decision makers, who are often not clear until late in production, and provides ways for them to be comfortably and effectively involved. In the end, SAM is a more inclusive process that has been optimized for instructional software development, which, in the end, is precisely what e-learning is.

Lie #3: Principles of Good Instructional Design Are Intuitive and Obvious

For years, instructional design professionals, especially those who focus on e-learning, have had to deal with what I might refer to as a little cluster of lies about their profession—anyone can do it, it's not even necessary, and other new technologies have become the primary mechanisms for learning and they don't require any design at all. This section will explore each.

Instead of diligently and intelligently applying what we know from research about how humans learn, many instructional design teams take a carefree approach, thinking there's too much puffery about something that's really quite simple. Our next lie about e-learning is that the principles of good instructional design are intuitive and obvious.

Regardless of delivery mode, producing instructional designs that effectively and efficiently produce performance excellence is a lot harder than it looks. Making matters worse, e-learning differs from instructor-led learning in what it can do and what it does well. Designers thus need to know which principles to apply where. There are many paths to becoming a good instructional designer, and some outstanding designers have little, if any, formal education on the underlying principles. Despite this, they are able to assess what makes a great learning experience and creatively design very effective instruction.

Sub-Lie #3a: Instructional Design Is Dead Because It's Unnecessary

Pundits, and others with an agenda, have been proclaiming the death of instructional design for years. Well, this may just be wishful thinking. They think (and sometimes say): "I don't know much about instructional design. Thank goodness we don't need it anyway."

We repeatedly see a desire for quick, easy solutions when it comes to instructional design and e-learning. Typically, although not always, those who are the loudest critics of the instructional design discipline are those who stand to benefit most by its demise—producers of new technologies, such as rapid authoring, template-based design, informal learning, social learning, and, more recently, gamification. They stand to benefit if their potential customers believe that their technologies render instructional design unnecessary. But this has rarely been the case, and the results almost never live up to the hype.

Sub-Lie #3b: Most People Are Learning Informally and That Doesn't Require Design

"Since we know that people in many organizations report that much of their training was informal, we just need to get out of the way." I hear this often in discussions weighing formal and informal learning methods. The complaints are the same: Formal learning programs are expensive, time-consuming to produce, boring, and ineffective. We're well advised to scrap formal learning and just sanction the informal learning that's going to happen anyway. Motivated people will figure out how to do their jobs; the others should just move on.

People with a high degree of technical expertise are usually very busy doing what they do best. When confronted with a request for some informal learning support, imagine a top performer having this internal dialogue: "Let's see. I'm really busy. What I can tell Jerry that will get him out of his situation now (and out of my hair)?" Top performers may not be good teachers and may not always be available when someone needs help. So while Jerry—stranded, stumped, and confused—is often drawn to the expert for direction, the expert may, in fact, be the least available and most expensive person to provide help. The expert may provide a temporary shortcut, put work on hold to mentor, or let a less-knowledgeable person figure out how to help. None of these are good outcomes.

Poor methods and improper or ineffective shortcuts easily propagate when skill building is left to informal methods. Efficiency and productivity drops, competitive abilities are not nourished, and training costs rise. Informal learning certainly has a role to play. But while a good substitute for poor formal learning, it's far from a good substitute for well-executed formal learning (Eraut 2004). It certainly isn't the panacea that some industry experts would have us believe.

Informal learning will not create itself. It needs design and direction to overcome its deficiencies. To succeed, it requires time management, training and certification of mentors, facilitated matchmaking of learners and mentors, aids to help learners know when they need guidance and where they should go to get it, and many other preparations. Such preparations can be implemented, of course, but informal learning doesn't become effective when formal learning is simply abandoned.

In fact, recognition that informal learning has its shortcomings was what demanded the development of a more formal approach to learning. Both approaches are necessary, but neither is sufficient, and they both require carefully designed foundations to ensure success.

How can we overcome the lies being told about the worthiness of instructional design, particularly in relation to e-learning? We need to recognize that instructional design is a profession. Just as with dentistry or plumbing or brain surgery, one takes quite a risk entrusting the work to those who aren't fully qualified and haven't demonstrated their ability to perform.

The Serious eLearning Manifesto (Allen, Dirksen, Quinn, and Thalheimer 2014) was recently created by a group of concerned e-learning veterans to offer guidance to those new to the field and to provide criteria that buyers of e-learning products (off-the-shelf or custom) should apply when developing requirements for their courseware or evaluating quality. It describes the characteristics of good e-learning, indicators of poorly designed e-learning, and principles to guide designers as they create e-learning programs.

When solely relying on informal or social learning, make sure that those needing help know how to identify and contact the best resources and make sure those giving help know how to provide effective support. And don't forget, good instructional designers can also help train experts in how to guide others.

Lie #4: E-Learning Is Impersonal and Inferior to Instructor-Led Learning

Some opponents of e-learning say that it doesn't have the eyes, ears, and empathy of human instructors. That it can't replicate the magic good instructors create in their classrooms. And that it's best to stick with the tried and true.

But the truth is some e-learning fulfills the promise of technology-assisted, individualized learning and produces spectacular results—sometimes even better than what a great instructor can achieve in a classroom. It can engage and mesmerize. It can produce irrepressible glee and appreciation. It can give every learner its full attention—something no instructor, no matter how good, can do.

E-learning replays consistently and reliably. It does what we tell it to do and only what we tell it to do. Once the logic is in place, it never varies because of illness, a lapse of memory, or a misstatement. It can match the pace that's best for each learner. It has infinite patience. It uses the same criteria to judge every learner's answer. It's available all day and every day. And it never forgets the learner's performance history, which it can draw on instantly.

E-learning is superior to instructor-led delivery because we can change it, knowing that the change will be carried out for every subsequent learner. We can systematically improve e-learning much more readily than instructor-led delivery, through application, feedback, and modification. Regardless of the effectiveness of an e-learning program, we can keep improving it until it meets our needs and, more important, our learners' needs. And once we have done that, we can count on it to achieve its goals consistently and fairly.

In the end, I think that e-learning is considered inferior because designers and implementers fail to plan and budget for revisions. They do not test out their first version, perhaps on a small group of learners, to determine its effectiveness and what can be improved. It's pretty simple, yet, somewhat inexplicably, rarely done.

Unfortunately, great results are too rare. And the risks are high because just as e-learning can earn superlatives, it can also result in staunch criticism. If learners like it, they talk about it, but if they don't like it, they talk about it even more. Effective uses tend to be very effective, while anything less tends to be painful and monotonous. Even when well-grounded principles of instruction and human learning are carefully applied, the resulting learning experience can be dreadful.

Some common mistakes to avoid in designing e-learning are:

> creating content-focused presentations ("text and next"), rather than well-considered, challenge-focused learning experiences

> omitting meaningful evaluation from the implementation plan

> not planning or budgeting for improvement iterations.

Even instructor-led delivery quickly becomes impersonal if the focus is simply on presenting information. With e-learning we can ensure that learners receive the appropriate instruction and practice by steering them clear of monotonously flipping through content pages and, instead, challenging them to perform tasks. If the learners perform well, they can skip ahead to content they find more interesting and helpful. If they need help, we can elaborate on the content that will be useful.

These are basic concepts that should characterize nearly all e-learning. But too often, e-learning misses the mark. The rapidly expanded use of e-learning has forced many people into becoming instructional designers, a role they have had very little professional preparation for. They have not had the opportunity to learn these concepts and thus focus on content presentations rather than learning experiences. To improve e-learning, companies must be willing to trust it to the people skilled in the art and science of instructional design.

Lie #5: Evaluating E-Learning Is Too Difficult and Expensive, So We Don't Need to Do It

Far too often I hear: "It's difficult and expensive to do impact or return-on-investment studies. We don't know how and we don't have the budget. And even if we did have the money, we'd be better off developing instruction on another topic than just checking to see if what we did works. And besides, if we got bad news, what would we do about it? It would just make our department look bad. No thanks!" But not all evaluation is difficult nor is it always expensive. And more important, evaluation is critical to successful e-learning.

Unlike more traditional forms of learning, meaningful evaluation methods can be incorporated directly into e-learning so it can adapt to learner needs, while also identifying where learning is and isn't happening. When designed well, e-learning continuously evaluates learner performance and progress to determine whether a learner needs more practice or if a learner is ready to advance to more challenging skills. Indeed, e-learning practitioners can't use learners' time efficiently and provide them with a beneficial experience if they aren't collecting data along the way. Although courseware can't directly measure post-training performance or the impact of on-the-job performance, it can ensure that learners are capable of the desired performance in the learning context.

How can you do this? By making sure that your e-learning has performance-sensitive branching capabilities that determine what each learner should do next. It shouldn't simply cruise through topics, assuming that exposure to the same content in the same way will be effective for all learners. It should accurately detect whether learners need alternative explanations or additional practice, have those resources available, and be able to use them according to individual needs. And it should not force capable people to study previously mastered content.

This approach delivers a substantial amount of information that can be a useful proxy for the information gathered from evaluation studies that measure on-the-job performance. So while calculating ROI is difficult under any circumstance, e-learning can provide concrete information about development costs and job performance, and help recover lost opportunity costs from the dramatic reduction in time spent learning. And that is without any of the additional work that is required for achieving the same goals with classroom learning.

Lie #6: E-Learning Must Be Offered in Small Morsels

Apparently, some believe that e-learning is so hard to digest that learners need it cut up in small pieces, lest they bite off more than they can chew. This lie is often reinforced by lengthy explanations that today's digital learners have little patience and very short attention spans. That the only way to connect to today's learners is to get in and get out quickly. In fact, some wonder whether we should even expect them to actually learn anything. And some suggest we just give learners checklists or online instructions to follow, because they're not going to be interested in putting in the time to learn anyway.

This willingness to throw in the towel—to blame learners for not being stimulated by boring e-learning and to not even try to build meaningful, memorable, and motivational learning experiences—continues to gain steam. It reinforces the lie that instructional design isn't necessary, particularly for e-learning.

Sure, the interest-sustaining novelty of e-learning wore off many years ago. But short segments are not necessarily the solution. Of course, if the e-learning is going to be painfully boring, most people would prefer it to be short. But we know from the long hours many people spend playing video games that people do have sufficient attention spans if sufficiently engaged. And we also know that to build complex skills, brief contact with learners is simply not enough.

When we individualize e-learning—adapt it to a learner's abilities by, for example, alternately raising and lowering the difficulty so that it demands concentration (as video games do)—learners will tune in for surprisingly long periods of time. And, not only will they enthusiastically endorse the learning method, but they will also recommend it to their friends.

Conclusion

We're always looking for the easy solution, especially, it seems, to avoid the hard work of instructional design or even education and training as a whole. But being competitive and succeeding in the learning market-place requires the right competencies, and this includes understanding e-learning. Time and again, e-learning has proved that it can be an extraordinary and economical means of achieving success.

But you must be wary of the many tempting pitfalls and misconceptions about e-learning. Here are the ones covered in this chapter:

> ➤ While technology may reduce the costs of instruction, you should apply some of the expected savings to improving the design and development of the courseware, or you may be saddled with ineffective learning products.

> ➤ Design methodologies have advanced—take SAM, for example—so instructional design is not nearly as hard or expensive as with ADDIE and other legacy models.

> ➤ Instructional design, especially for e-learning, requires developed expertise; rapid authoring and templates speed up development but don't supplant good design. Informal learning has a role to play, but formal learning may be necessary when experts are not available to help mentor learners.

> ➤ E-learning has its limitations, but it can provide levels of individual adaptability that are unmanageable in classroom settings.

> ➤ Evaluation within e-learning is necessary to deliver individualized experiences, so claiming that it is too difficult or expensive is not an excuse. At the same time, e-learning can provide a great deal of information about development costs, reductions in delivery costs, and projections about on-the-job performance that are simply not available with other forms of learning.

➤ When e-learning is engaging and valuable, learners prefer longer sessions that go deeper in substance, not just brief interactions with the content.

I hope this chapter has prepared you to counter all those worrisome lies and you're ready to reap the incredible advantages of e-learning.

References

Allen, M.W., and R. Sites. 2012. *Leaving ADDIE for SAM: An Agile Model for Developing the Best Learning Experiences.* Alexandria, VA: ASTD Press.

Allen, M.W., J. Dirksen, C. Quinn, W. Thalheimer. 2014. "The Manifesto." Serious eLearning Manifesto. http://elearningmanifesto.org.

Branson, R.K., G.T. Rayner, J.L. Cox, J.P. Furman, and F.J. King. 1975. *Interservice Procedures for Instructional Systems Development* (Task V Final Report). Tallahassee: Florida State University, Center for Educational Technology.

Eraut, M. 2004. "Informal Learning in the Workplace." *Studies in Continuing Education* 26(2): 247–273.

Recommended Reading

Cross, J. 2011. *Informal Learning: Rediscovering the Natural Pathways That Inspire Innovation and Performance.* San Francisco: Pfeiffer.

Lies About Learning Technology

Elliott Masie

L ies are everywhere when the conversation turns to learning technology. They are natural and, perhaps, unavoidable effects of the excitement and buzz around new technologies. Something new is invented or discovered, and we start to dream of innovation and improvement. But the lies go even deeper when it comes to learning technology.

The lies about learning technology have had some fascinating—and disastrous—effects. We've adopted immature technologies long before they are ready, often causing confusion and leading to disappointment over undelivered promises. We've implemented learning technologies before learning methods for using them have been developed, which leads to little or no impact. We've failed to test new technologies against current approaches, sometimes leaving the organization without any evidence of success (or failure). We've bought into overpriced and overstated new technologies; few learning products enter the market at an affordable level, and their value is often exaggerated.

We've fallen in love with buzzwords like "mobile learning" without there being models that work with today's technologies. We've embraced technology-leveraged approaches, such as big learning data, without having the skills in the learning organization to fully understand or implement the changes identified through the data analysis. And we've created a usability void by showing rapid affection for technologies before system-ically assessing their impact on users.

Many players in our changing field tell, retell, or at least tolerate these learning technology lies. Learning technology providers, IT departments, learning departments, learning magazines and analysts, and even users—they all lie about learning technology.

And for the record, I'm guilty of spreading some of these lies. I've spent more than 30 years covering the world of learning and technology, and my track record includes some amazing whoppers along the way. While I may have gotten it right when we first started to use "e-learning" in the mid-1990s to describe the application of the emerging Internet to computer-based training, I whiffed on my excitement over the impact of the virtual world of Second Life. I imagined classrooms across the world shifting into digital, animated meeting places. I even spent $60,000 on a Second Life MASIE Center and a digitally enhanced Elliott avatar. Yes, even I have told some big—but well-intentioned—lies along the way.

Affordance—A Key Phrase

The one term that could help frame our thinking about learning technol-ogy is "affordance." It has been applied to design and technology, but it can also be adapted to learning technology. Affordance is the potential or actual ability of a technology to supply a designer, organization, or learner with an expanded skill in the learning process. It can be a powerful way to honor the flow of new technologies, while acknowledging that we may not yet know how they can enhance the learning process.

Using affordance as a framework can provide structure to how an organization approaches each new technology or learning technology methodology:

> ➤ **Designer affordance.** How would this learning technology provide affordances in designing a learning activity? Would it help make the design faster, more agile, more adaptive, more reusable, more user friendly, or more shareable?

> **Organization affordance.** How would this learning technology provide affordances to the organization in developing, delivering, assessing, and managing learning? Would it make learning management more responsive, less costly, more enterprise ready, more easily updatable, or more learner adaptive? Does it yield a benefit for the organization as a customer of the technology?

> **Learner affordance.** How would this learning technology provide affordances to learners while they learn? Would it make the learning faster, easier, deeper, more rigorous, more supportive of performance, or more portable?

Affordances force us to ask deeper and more specific questions about how an exciting new or improved technology will affect designers, managers, learners, and other stakeholders in the learning process. Sure, the ads and articles about learning technologies describe improvements or enhancements. But excitement often overrides looking at the technologies from a critical affordance perspective. We must overcome our excitement in order to make wise business decisions about which learning technologies to invest in.

Let's now examine the lies being told about new learning technologies, particularly smartphones, learning apps, our old models and new technologies, and massive open online courses (MOOCs).

Lie #1: Smartphones Will Radically Change Learning

On June 29, 2007, Apple introduced the iPhone, the first device that would allow users to move their fingers across a handheld screen to access information. This triggered many thoughts and fantasies among learning professionals of how smartphones could offer infinite affordances to radically change learning.

I fantasized about how the iPhone could be a personalized learning world—a handheld device for every worker that enabled content, performance support, collaboration, and more. And I predicted that all of this would be just a year or two away. I imagined an affordance and a timeline that did not resonate with reality.

I imagined the death of the laptop, because the iPhone fit easily in pockets and purses. One affordance that continues to evolve is the "phablet," a combination between phone and tablet. I recalled the introduction and excitement around earlier handheld devices, including Newton, Slate, and Palm. But they didn't easily apply to workplace technology because of technology, business, design, and even branding issues that slowed workplace adoption.

After I picked up my new iPhone on my way to deliver a speech at West Point, I passed it around to several military and police officers in attendance, asking them to imagine how it might be used. Dozens of ideas flowed about how a soldier or police officer might use it, including being able to deliver mobile courses easily and seamlessly to the iPhone. I left the speech thinking that the iPhone would radically change work and learning for the military and police—and soon.

Smartphones were no doubt radical innovations. But have they radically changed learning? That is still an open question wrapped up in some lies:

> Smartphones have taken seven years to evolve, adding more functionality along the way, including cell-based Internet, two-sided cameras, GPS, and higher definition screens. Affordances have increased as each of these functions has been added.

> Mobile learning was announced as the future of learning when smartphones were launched. I remember 12 press releases from companies debuting "world-changing" e-learning courses as mobile learning courses. Taking a course on a three-inch screen in nine-point type, with limited graphical ability and restricted input options, might be interesting, but it has been far from world changing.

➤ Google searches by learners from their smartphones were missing from most of the early reports about mobile learning. It took time and increased bandwidth to harvest search as a key affordance.

➤ Enterprise affordances from smartphones were blocked right from the start. Organizations were frustrated in their desire to allow secure access to workers within enterprise security frameworks.

➤ BYOD (bring your own device) issues took years to address. At many organizations, workers have distinctly different access on their desktops compared with their smartphones, often requiring two searches on two devices to get a learning perspective from both internal and external knowledge sources.

Are mobile devices going to play a larger role in workplace learning? Of course. But technologies and methodologies take time to evolve, and our ability to envision and harvest the affordances for designers, managers, and learners requires experimentation, analysis, collaboration, benchmarking, and evidence. So allow me to summarize our experience with leveraging smartphones for workplace learning.

Smartphones:

➤ were exciting from the start

➤ had unlimited futures imagined

➤ were announced as ready and fully able to provide learning affordances in 2007

➤ experienced many learning innovation failures related to readiness and usability

➤ appeared to be more useful at home than in the workplace

➤ forced changes to enterprise security and business processes

➤ evolved with time, reflection, and experience

➤ may even be more exciting in 2015 than they were in 2007.

Lie #2: Learning Apps Are the Future for Workplace Learning

With the advent of smartphones came apps, which many learning professionals and organizations have promoted as the future for workplace learning. However, it remains to be seen whether this pronouncement about learning apps will eventually be more truth or lie.

The average smartphone user has downloaded some 40 apps, most of which were free or purchased for under $10 (Sawers 2012). These apps provide users affordances for travel, news monitoring, communication, gaming, hiring a car service, and much more. But what about apps for learning? There are translation apps for accessing literature and communication from global sources, note-storage apps that allow cutting and saving snippets from websites, and collaboration apps that allow real-time communication with teammates in other locations. Many of these are what I would call *learning apps*, in that they provide improved and expanded capabilities for learners in specific situations.

Yet, there are not many learning apps in the corporate marketplace. In 2014, I visited hundreds of booths at the Association for Talent Development's International Conference & EXPO in Washington, D.C., looking for some low-priced-per-user learning apps. And while there were loads of $100,000–$10,000,000 learning systems, I couldn't find a single $1.99 app that would help a learner acquire a new skill or develop a new competency.

Interestingly, learning apps have popped up in other learning fields:

➤ **K–12 education.** Kahn Academy and TED Ed have offered apps and mobile access that provide affordances for teachers, by helping them create custom lessons, and learners, by allowing them to build and participate in communities around content.

➤ **Higher education.** Companies are producing learning apps that provide affordances for college students (such as RescueTime and RefMe). Others are in the emerging MOOC space. (More about MOOCs later.)

➤ **Health and wellness.** Weight Watchers has radically redesigned its services around online and mobile apps.

In reality, learning apps are just starting to emerge—with some hesitancy—in corporate learning. This may be for several reasons. They're too cheap: Learning programs offered for free or very inexpensively represent a threat to the higher-priced content providers. They're too open: Learning apps that provide more affordances to the learner, including using nontraditional resources, are perhaps somewhat threatening to highly controlled organizations. And they're too new: Organizations don't have good usability models for assessing their efficiency or effectiveness on workplace productivity or time to competency.

But the learning industry has a wonderful opportunity to experiment, benchmark, and explore innovation in the world of learning apps as well as other areas.

Lie #3: We Can Apply Our Old Models to the New Technologies

Another important lie about learning technology is that we immediately understand new technologies and can easily imagine the ways in which we can apply old models to new platforms. Yet that instant analysis may not yield real innovation.

Think back to when webinar technology emerged. In the mid-1990s, the speed and functionality of webinar platforms, most of which were still in beta, was exciting—and yet limited. The first webinar affordances to develop were about replicating lecture- and classroom-based PowerPoint delivery to learners in distributed locations. In other words, the affordances were distributing lectures to a wider audience and not having to travel. Not exactly groundbreaking.

As is often the case with new technologies, we take our models from the previous technology and apply them to the new one—television was radio with a picture for many years. But as learning technologies evolve, there is a window for exploring new and different affordances for designers, organizations, and learners. Webinar tools today provide for more video, interaction windows, and engagement capabilities, but most webinars are far from engaging for learners, and many are still real-time lectures with the occasional opportunity for audience participation. The lie is thus not in the learning technology tool, but in our slowness to discover and experiment with new affordances for design and delivery. As a result, webinars are the fastest growing element of technology-based learning delivery, but which also allow for the highest levels of learner multitasking and distraction.

The lies about learning technology do not come just from technology providers—they also come from our own self-limiting design perspectives. Learners themselves are redesigning many of our webinars by participating while simultaneously working on other tasks (and eating lunch) or by not showing up at all (many webinars have a no-show rate as high as 40 percent of preregistered learners). Learners are adapting for their own affordances. Perhaps managers and designers need to take a fresh, evidence-based look at webinars to discover new design and delivery models with increased affordances for everyone.

Affordances are really in the mind of the beholder. Each player in the learning world sees a technology from his own perspective, with his own affordances. We often don't apply an industry-wide perspective to learning technology. The learner may view it as a personalization tool, the designer may view it as a depth and alignment tool, and the manager may view it as a cost-avoidance tool.

Our learners are agile. In fact, they are more agile than most learning designers and managers. To keep up, we need to create an evidence-based, usability-rich approach for exploring each new learning technology, rather than continuing to apply our old, often-out-of-date approaches.

Lie #4: MOOCs Can Be Easily Translated From Higher Education to the Workplace

Beware of some of the new acronyms coming our way in learning technology. Several letters forming a cute new term, like *MOOC*, often reflect a new technology or a new learning methodology that has hit a level of shared curiosity. We need to be both curious and smart.

MOOCs are high on my radar at the moment—four letters, each exploring an affordance or extension of learning design and delivery:

> ➤ **M—Massive.** These programs allow for access to hundreds, thousands, or even hundreds of thousands of learners, without radically expanding the number of teachers or coaches.

> ➤ **O—Open.** These programs use open content, where much of the material comes from external and often free sites like TED and YouTube, and offer open access, where learners of all types can enroll. For example, a leadership program open to all employees, not just those who are currently, or expected to become, managers.

> ➤ **O—Online.** These programs facilitate learning primarily through online content, context, collaboration, and assessment. The learner can access a MOOC from anywhere, anytime, and with personalized scheduling.

> ➤ **C—Course, community, credit, collaboration, or certification.** These programs can serve a variety of different purposes for learners, whether it is acquiring credits for a degree or earning a certificate to widen their knowledge base.

MOOCs are new. They're popular with many in higher education. They're presented as a disruptive force in learning. And they're perceived as a technology for learning innovators to watch. But there is confusion in translating them from higher education to the workplace. While colleges see MOOCs as not only open-access courses, but also pathways to awarding academic credits, many employers see them more as focused on providing a community of content or leading to a badge or certification.

So how should learning directors and professionals approach MOOCs for the corporate workplace? First, a few lies that you will hear about MOOCs:

> ➤ They work great (tens of thousands take a program with limited costs and faculty time). Or they don't work (80 percent of participants never complete them).

> ➤ They can be purchased for employees from branded universities at a relatively low cost.

> ➤ They are highly attractive to workers, who can learn based on their own needs and schedules.

> ➤ They are very collaborative; learners help one another in online communities. Or they are not collaborative, because online community designs are not scalable without leaders and facilitators.

> ➤ They are the future of learning technology. Or they are just a hot item.

In many ways, each of these items isn't a lie, but rather just a slice of the MOOC conversation. MOOCs are, thus, a great example of how learning leaders and organizations should rise above the hype.

To do this, I recommend that learning professionals learn more about learning and MOOCs. They should take a few MOOCs from colleges, for-profit businesses, and other sources. Find out what works and what doesn't from a learner's perspective.

They should deconstruct the acronym and ask if they can implement a stretched version of a single letter, without the full MOOC. Is there a way to add open content to existing face-to-face and e-learning programs? Is there a way to take a program from small to massive?

They should look at MOOCs not just as the impetus for new learning assets, but also as a trigger for reducing or ending some current offerings. If MOOCs work, what can learning organizations stop delivering? If MOOCs work, what can designers stop designing?

And they should evaluate usability and listen to their audience—the learners. Some learners may enjoy MOOCs that are structured like a multiweek class, building toward a final at the end. But others may want to have all the sessions ready for them to take at their own pace, perhaps even in one gigantic weekend MOOC marathon. How do learners evolve or shift their learning behaviors in a MOOC?

So, take that term *MOOC*, along with all its excitement, and explore it for workplace affordances. Beware the supplier who tells you that they have it solved and are the "leading number one creator of MOOCs, with 72 percent of the Fortune 500 as customers." Some of that might be true, but you want to partner with explorers and evidence-based designers for this process. I still don't know the answer, for example, to these questions:

> ➤ If 3,000 people sign up for a MOOC and only 300 finish, are the other 2,700 failing, or are they getting just enough of what they want? Some would argue that a MOOC is like an article in *USA Today*, where some will read just the headline, others the first paragraph, still others the whole article, and some will go online for even more depth.

> ➤ Are MOOCs about completion or learner-directed participation?

And I'm sure that I don't know the answers to several other questions, which I also don't yet know.

Learning leaders need to embrace the excitement behind MOOCs and explore what workplace affordances they may provide. But they need to acknowledge that different organizations require different affordances—that there is no one-size-fits-all model. Don't be afraid to deconstruct the acronym and apply the letters you need to your workplace learning.

More Lies About Learning Technology

The conversation around the lies about learning technology could go on for days and fill its own book. So let's quickly review some other important learning technologies in the corporate learning field and the lies surrounding them.

Video. More web activity means that learners are consuming more learning materials through short videos, and learning leaders are designing more courses with video content. And more content is flowing from user-created videos. But most learning systems are not ready or cannot adapt to video content. Many organizations have to place their videos outside their learning management systems and are unable to collect critical data, such as at what point do users close out of a video. Learning technology providers must rapidly accept the growth of video and provide better tools and systems to organizations.

Search. Learners want to search for answers. They want to search content in the wide reaches of the organization, even for older Power-Points that might just be on a co-worker's laptop. One of the lies from IT is that they are providing the search capabilities that learners need.

Big learning data. There is a big appetite for big data in the learning world, based on high-level executives' ever-increasing interest in analytics. Beware of big learning data. (I say this even though I authored the ATD book on the topic.) The caution is to not fall for a lightweight view of a very deep topic. In many ways, big learning data is a learning technology that can provide affordances for designers, managers, and learners. Do some research and then sit with learning professionals in other organizations to figure out which aspects of big learning data can be leveraged now and which may be available downstream. And be sure to keep the learner as one of the top customers for big data.

Application programming interfaces (APIs) and interactivity. Some day learning technologies will just work together, when colleagues can participate in a meeting through Skype, WebEx, Telepresence, and FaceTime, along with a few by phone. These technologies should work together. It gets even more frustrating if an organization wants to integrate multiple technologies, especially when suppliers say that it is all possible. What learning leaders need are APIs that allow for the low-cost integration and connectivity of multiple learning technologies.

BYOD. Organizations and technology providers, including mobile and cell companies, need to find ways for workers to use privately owned devices in more secure and corporately comfortable ways. Imagine having a button on a smart device that flips the use from home to work through, for example, a GPS location allowing for at-work access.

Conclusion

I'd like to advocate for the creation of a public list of "we were wrong" statements. Innovation requires that we fail our way to success. Many of us will make pronouncements about learning technology that will become lies only through the passage of time and experimentation. I was wrong about Second Life. I was wrong about the speed of laptop demise. And I'm sure I was wrong about many other learning technologies. Let's do a better job of conducting and sharing our predictions and statements about learning technology—the good and the bad.

Some Future Learning Technologies

Here are five learning technologies that I am experimenting with as well as seeking the affordances they may provide:

> **Drones.** My four-blade helicopter drone has a GoPro high-definition camera that takes amazing video from hundreds of feet above the ground. I am seeking affordances for how it might be used for insurance inspector training or other applications.

> **Wearables.** I have my Google Glass, Nike Band, and smartwatches. I bet these devices and other wearables could yield some incredible affordances for learners—perhaps not yet, but they are intriguing and deserve experimentation.

> **Neuroscience sensors.** We are exploring the role that neuroscience sensors might play by providing feedback on brain scans and the physical reactions of learners to new content.

> ➤ **Crowd-sourced design.** Imagine harnessing 100 colleagues from around the enterprise to do a rapid, crowd-sourced design of a learning activity.

> ➤ **Multilanguage webinar.** When learners from five countries, all of whom speak different languages, are on a webinar together, how does language translation provide an affordance?

Will any of these technologies and methodologies provide real affordances to designers, managers, and learners? Time and experimentation will tell. I am excited about each one, but I will try to contain my excitement. Time to be a bit more careful with lies about learning technology.

Reference

Sawers, P. 2012. "Nielsen: US Smartphones Have an Average of 41 Apps Installed, Up From 32 Last Year." The Next Web, May 12. http://thenextweb.com/insider/2012/05/16/nielsen-us-smartphones-have-an-average-of-41-apps-installed-up-from-32-last-year.

Part IV

Wrap-Up

10

Lies About Learning Pronouncements

Larry Israelite

I started my career in the field of learning and development in the early 1980s, working for a company that produced a high-end computer-based training system. At the time, we were one of several commercial enterprises that spawned from considerable investments in advanced research and development funded by the National Science Foundation and the military. The goal was to use computer technology to supplement (replace) classroom instruction.

Even in those days there was plenty of hype about the potential for computer-based training. Articles were written, papers were presented, and pronouncements were made—computer-based training will revolutionize classroom learning as we know it. Sound familiar?

This phenomenon didn't start in the early 1980s. In fact, I recall something that occurred in the mid-1960s that predicted the experience I had almost 20 years later. I arrived on my first day of ninth grade only to find televisions hanging in every classroom. Instructional television was going to revolutionize public education as we knew it. But as it turned out, programming was complicated to produce and expensive to purchase, and teachers who were effective in the classroom weren't so much on television. It didn't take long to figure out that instructional television could be useful in some circumstances but that it wasn't going to revolutionize learning.

To distill this issue down to its very essence, I would say we are suckers for a good pronouncement. They sound good, they give us hope, they are often made by people or institutions we respect, and they are hard to resist. But they also sometimes lead us to do things we later regret.

While going through some old files, I found a diagram I created in 1982. It shows what I described then as "the cycle of failure," our all too common experience when we accept pronouncements without proper evaluation (Figure 10-1). To draw it again today, the words might change slightly, but the sentiment would be the same. And I find it both amusing and disheartening that not much has changed in the intervening years. We still tend to invest (emotionally and financially) in approaches, methods, technologies, and tools that don't deliver the value they claim. We then live with the consequences of our misplaced confidence and enthusiasm and start all over again.

Figure 10-1. The Cycle of Failure

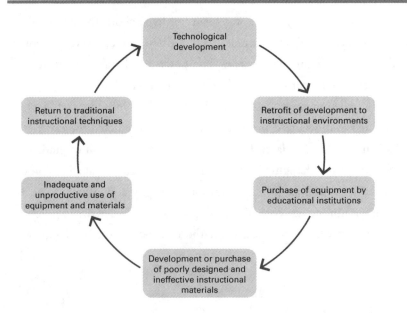

In this chapter, I will explore some pronouncements about learning that have had a major influence on the field of learning and development. What do I mean by pronouncement? For starters, it's a formal or authoritative announcement or declaration. But I'd like to add that a pronouncement is made by someone who is in a position of respect and authority or who exudes a high degree of confidence in what he is saying. My goal is to make explicit some of the more interesting "truths" we've heard in the past—and, in turn, to change how we respond to these in the future.

Pronouncement #1: E-Learning Will Revolutionize Training and Replace Classroom Education

As early as the mid-1980s, people started to predict the end of the classroom or, at least, to imagine a vastly different learning landscape. First, it was computer-based training or computer-assisted instruction. This was followed by interactive video (12-inch disc), multimedia CD-ROMs, videoconference technology, and the Internet. Many people were convinced that the Internet, with all its wonderful features and capabilities, would enable e-learning to replace the classroom experience. Bricks-and-mortar classrooms and training centers would become a thing of the past.

Before the availability of web-based video, people relied heavily on the virtual classroom. This technology, now available at almost no cost from hundreds of cloud vendors, allows learners to see instructors and watch their material in real time. This was just as good as being in a classroom—at least in theory.

At that time, we ignored the fact that much of the learning that takes place in a classroom involves interaction with other learners. So the early online virtual learning programs started to use discussion rooms and other tools to bring students together. Many even created breakout rooms where people could go to study or practice.

This virtual model still works pretty well. But it can't replace being together in the same space. And it seems the more technology we have, the more we crave to put it away, just sit down, and talk with one another. We have a certain ability to connect and interact face to face, which technology can't fully replicate. So even great video classrooms can't replace the need for classroom experiences. Note how Deloitte, McDonald's, GE, Unilever, and many other major corporations have recently built beautiful (bricks-and-mortar) corporate universities exactly for this reason.

While training continues to move online (today more than 30 percent of all corporate instructor hours are spent online; Bersin by Deloitte 2014), more than 50 percent of training is still spent in real classrooms, face-to-face with students. Clearly, the physical classroom remains a very important element of learning.

Each year will bring new and seemingly tradition-shattering learning technologies—tools that are more expressive (Google Hangouts, for example). But classrooms aren't going anywhere anytime soon. Sure, what we do in classrooms may change (such as the flipped classroom), but we will still need classrooms with live real-time teachers for years to come. It turns out that we just like to spend time with one another, occupying the same space, interacting in real time, and being able to reach out and touch someone.

All of this said, it appears that technical training—meaning training consumed by software developers, IT administrators, and creative professionals—may have reached the tipping point with regard to replacing classroom learning with e-learning. There are, literally, tens of thousands of very high-quality programs available that cover an almost endless array of topics. The fact that most of these programs are highly modularized, which enables users to focus only on topics that interest them or will be useful for them, only serves to increase the popularity of this learning alternative. And perhaps more important, these programs are available directly to learners, completely eliminating enterprise control and oversight. As a result, surveys like the one just referenced may not capture this significant shift in approach. So, while it may, in fact, be true that e-learning really is revolutionizing training and replacing classroom education for technical subjects, it also is true that we have a very long and complex row to hoe when considering other content domains.

Pronouncement #2: Gamification Will Radically Change Corporate Learning

Learning leaders have also made many pronouncements about gamification in recent years, particularly about how it will radically change corporate learning. Remember Second Life? Many companies invested in this technology believing that our entire learning experience would turn into a game. And while gamification has become a crucial part of our online experience, the suggestion that learning as a game will transform learning has proved false. Instead, gamification has morphed into features and practices (affordances) embedded into many Internet applications.

Consider how gamification features now appear in social networks like Facebook, LinkedIn, and Twitter. Most other providers of apps and tools give people points, social cues, personal profiles, quests, reminders, and other forms of gaming that help hook people on their applications. Gamification is, truly, ubiquitous.

In learning, games and gaming are nothing new. Many of our earliest learning experiences involve receiving rewards for completing lessons or gold stars for perfect attendance. A gold star isn't that much different from the badge you receive when you post to a social collaboration site or complete a learning module. And even the slider bar that shows progress or points received for completing a section of an online course qualifies as gamification. In classrooms, we have used games for as long as I can remember—to engage, motivate, and stimulate learners.

Gamification can play a meaningful role in learning. But we should treat it the same as we treat other instructional techniques intended to improve effectiveness. Games are tools in the instructional designer tool-kit, not the toolkit itself. So learning and development professionals need to remember to use them appropriately.

But there is a dark side to the proliferation of gamification. Take LinkedIn, for example. My profile page lists the skills for which I've been endorsed and shows little pictures of the contacts whose endorsements I've received. That's all very nice. Except for the fact that I have not met or ever worked with many of my endorsers, so they are in no position to fairly judge my capabilities. In the end, I'm largely suspicious of the endorsements other people receive, thus diminishing them as a recruiting tool. So I am forced to ask, "Does this process have any value?"

Pronouncement #3: Mobile Learning Will Replace [Insert Other Forms of Learning Here]

I can't tell you how many times I have heard people say that they need to deliver their content through mobile devices. For many years that was both impossible and ill advised. Before smartphones and tablets, mobile devices were completely ill equipped for high-fidelity learning. Sure, learners could scroll through some text, attempt to look at very small graphics, listen to some audio files, and answer a few questions, but that was about it. Mobile learning was nothing more than a pipe dream.

But the iPhone, the iPad, and the Android operating system have dramatically changed the mobile environment. People of all ages spend hours on their mobile devices, finding information by searching on Google, browsing YouTube, or downloading any of the hundreds of apps and tools with content-designed specifically for mobile. And, of course, learning occurs.

There were two lies associated with the pronouncement about mobile learning. The first pronouncement was made far too early, long before the technology could actually deliver the well-designed, highly engaging experiences possible today. In 2015, most suppliers develop their programs so they run on all devices—desktop and mobile. And since we now spend 60 percent of our online time on a mobile platform (Lipsman 2014), it is clear that mobile has arrived.

The second lie involves what has almost become a learning anathema —the word "replace." During the past 33 years, no new learning technology that I am aware of has ever fully replaced another. So while mobile learning will undoubtedly play a large role in learning, it likely won't replace anything either, in the same way that e-learning never fully replaced classroom learning, pundit pronouncements notwithstanding. And we run the risk that, given the hype about mobile, designers will feel pressured to deliver solutions on mobile devices that have no business being there.

In the end, mobile has taken its rightful and, perhaps, long overdue place in the instructional designer toolkit. And ongoing advances in technology are likely to increase its importance as the tool of choice for addressing specific learning needs. But mobile won't be replacing anything—at least from a learning perspective—anytime soon.

Pronouncement #4: Learning and Development Strategy Should Be Based on the 70-20-10 Model

People love simple models. And for better or worse the 70-20-10 model has captured the imagination of talent management professionals everywhere. The ratio suggests that people learn 70 percent from experience, 20 percent from other people, and 10 percent from formal training. And this model does have some validity. It makes sense that doing things results in more learning than talking about, hearing about, or reading about them does. But as near as I can tell, there is little sound empirical evidence backing up the ratio.

The real value of the model is that it depicts a comprehensive example of blended learning, a phrase that has been part of the learning vernacular since the turn of the century. Originally, blended learning described a program of both individual and group learning. For example, it included one or more e-learning modules and some form of classroom experience (live or virtual). Some of the programs designed this way were quite effective, but others were not.

The 70-20-10 model pushes the blended concept even further. Suppose a blended program included a formal learning component that was followed by specific on-the-job assignments, during which learners attempted to apply what they had learned. Then suppose we add a series of structured conversations with managers and peers about how they see the learners applying their new skills. Without over-engineering the exact time allocation, you can imagine something that approximates the 70-20-10 structure.

Within the 70-20-10 model, learning leaders often forget to account for reflection, even though research has concluded that it is critical to learning (Di Stefano et al. 2014). Learning from direct experience can be more effective if coupled with reflection—that is, attempting to synthesize, abstract, and articulate the key lessons taught by experience. And reflection builds one's self-efficacy, which in turn translates into higher rates of learning. So just having an experience doesn't mean that you will learn all you can from it unless you also reflect on it. And that is more difficult than it might seem.

When we apply 70-20-10 as a rule—when it drives strategic decisions, including staffing and budgets—it can force us to abandon those things that have proved necessary for learning to occur: motivated learners, an environment conducive to learning, relevant content, well-designed instruction, meaningful practice, and opportunities to reflect. And, simply, no good can come from that.

Pronouncement #5: Search-Enabled "Fingertip Learning" Will Replace More Traditional Forms of Learning

Search is a marvelous invention. Not a day goes by during which I don't conduct at least a dozen Internet searches for all kinds of information. Many searches are for work, some are for pleasure, and some are for the information I need to run my life (such as, is my train running on time?). Access to this type of information has become indispensable.

Several years ago, the phrase "fingertip learning" emerged as a means of describing the impact that search was having (or could have) on how we learn. It developed out of the very thing search provides—instantaneous access to almost anything. The underlying theory was simple: If we search for something, find it, and act on it, learning has occurred. But are we not just confusing fingertip information with actual learning?

There are many theories about how learning occurs or how to create environments that promote or facilitate learning. So my question, then, is very simple: When I search, does learning occur? Did it result in "a persisting change in human performance or performance potential" (Driscoll 2004)? Let's consider an example.

Like most people, I occasionally forget to periodically save my documents. And for reasons I can't explain, I lose my latest versions. As result, I have to frantically look for the backups or temporary files that exist somewhere on my computer. So I enter a Google search for something like: "finding lost word files on my Mac." Half a second later, I start to pick through the 2.4 million results to find the one that will best help me. In most cases, I find the information I need, follow the procedure, and recover my files.

The question is whether I learned anything from that experience—other than that I need to save my documents more often. For the most part, the answer is no. I certainly have not memorized the file-recovery process, which doesn't worry me because the next time I can just conduct the same search or bookmark the webpage I need. So while search absolutely helped me solve my problem, it did not result in a persisting change in performance. It was not a learning device.

What my search actually gave me was fingertip information, and that is almost always incredibly valuable. The information I received enabled me to solve my problem quickly and efficiently. In essence, Google, Bing, and other search engines have become the world's most powerful and comprehensive performance support systems. What they do so incredibly well is provide us with instantaneous access to information, pictures, videos, and other materials that might help us learn.

But it isn't that simple. Search engines fail to provide context. Suppose we want to learn more about Alzheimer's disease (5.5 million hits in just more than a quarter of a second). We could start by going to the Alzheimer's Association website. Or instead, we could read Wikipedia to get some background and develop a plan of attack from there. But we must develop the plan, and we probably don't know enough to do that very effectively.

All this is not to say that search engines don't play an incredibly important role in learning. They do. But their role is based on what they do best—finding and displaying information quickly and efficiently. I suspect that Pluralsight, edX, Skillshare, and other online content providers would agree that search engines contribute greatly to their individual and collective success. So while it's inaccurate to say that search-enabled fingertip learning will replace more traditional forms of training, it's certainly true that search enables learning and has become an indispensable partner in the learning value chain.

Pronouncement #6: The Kirkpatrick Model Rules

In the early 1990s, I worked in the educational services department of a large computer company that offered training to employees and customers. Each quarter the vice president would hold a meeting to report on two results metrics—"butts in seats" and revenue. If both went up quarter over quarter, we were happy; if they didn't, we weren't. Those meetings sent a very clear message about what really mattered.

In 1994, Donald Kirkpatrick published his seminal book on measuring learning, *Evaluating Training Programs*. His four-level measurement model became the industry standard for evaluating the overall quality of the training offered in organizations everywhere. Kirkpatrick forced us to think differently about the questions we asked and how we asked them. We started to adjust our fixation on how many people attended a program and increase our concern about whether their attendance actually mattered. Did they learn anything? Did they apply it in their work? Did it have a positive influence on outcomes or results?

This shift to a more structured approach to the evaluation of learning has been, and continues to be, a slow process for many reasons:

> ➤ Lack of skill on the part of learning and development professionals—writing good measures of knowledge, skill, application, and impact is time-consuming and difficult; interpreting and acting on the results is, too.

> ➤ Organizational indifference or unwillingness to do the work required to identify the right metrics and collect the necessary data.

> ➤ Lack of institutional rewards for participating in a comprehensive measurement strategy—conducting evaluations, taking tests, and filling out observational checklists take time. And if employees and managers don't believe there are any consequences for not participating, their interest in doing so diminishes greatly.

My point isn't that the Kirkpatrick model, either the original or recently updated version, doesn't work. To the contrary, I think they both make sense. I just think that they require a level of skill, discipline, and institutional will that is hard to find.

In addition, the world of learning differs drastically from the one Kirkpatrick experienced during most of his working life. Companies offer thousands of courses—classroom based, e-learning, internally developed, vendor provided, live, and virtual. And if we had the time to do the research, we probably would learn that average usage is very low and that we have almost no data that answer the very basic questions of value: Which programs drive the most value (assuming you can define it)? Which elements of these programs are the best? How can we make the best programs even better? On what objective basis can we eliminate, rationalize, or reduce the clutter in our training offerings? And we haven't even touched how to measure the value of the vast content available outside our corporate firewalls.

Despite widespread understanding of the Kirkpatrick framework, it really doesn't answer these questions. Perhaps the answer is in finding the right way to ask another question: How highly would you recommend this course to your peers? This question alone would tell us whether a course adds value and whether employees believe they are learning valuable things from it. Capturing, collecting, and analyzing answers to this simple question could be extremely useful.

Don't mistake this for a claim that the Kirkpatrick model holds no value. Instead, I am suggesting that the learning world of 2015 requires much more. Just as the sophistication of the instructional design toolkit has improved since the 1990s, so too must the approaches, methods, and tools we use to evaluate learning and learning outcomes.

Conclusion

On almost any day, learning professionals can visit a website, look at a professional journal, read a pundit's blog, or leaf through some new industry book and discover a new and exciting pronouncement. It's been that way for as long as I have been in this profession, and I don't expect it to change any time soon. All we can do is take everything with a grain of salt, and try our best to figure out what these pronouncements really mean, how they might help us, and what we have to watch out for. And, above all else, don't be afraid to push back when the little voice in your head is saying that something is too good to be true, or that you've heard it before.

References

Bersin by Deloitte. 2014. *The Corporate Learning Factbook 2014: Benchmarks, Trends, and Analysis of the U.S. Training Market.* Oakland, CA: Bersin by Deloitte.

Di Stefano, G., F. Gino, G. Pisano, and B. Staats. 2014. "Learning by Thinking: How Reflection Aids Performance." Working Paper, Harvard University.

Driscoll, M.P. 2004. *Psychology of Learning for Instruction.* 3rd ed. Boston: Allyn and Bacon.

Kirkpatrick, D.L. 1994. *Evaluating Training Programs: The Four Levels.* San Francisco: Berrett-Koehler.

Lipsman, A. 2014. "Major Mobile Milestones in May: Apps Now Drive Half of All Time Spent on Digital." Insights (blog), comScore, June 25. www.comscore.com/Insights/Blog/Major-Mobile-Milestones-in-May -Apps-Now-Drive-Half-of-All-Time-Spent-on-Digital.

Final Words: Parting Shots

Larry Israelite

I often start these projects with some idea of how I would like to end them. And I had planned to name this last chapter something like "Some Truths About Learning." That's how I ended *Lies About Learning*, and I figured it would work for this one too. But then I started reading and working with the chapters, and my plan started to change. Allow me to take you through my thought process.

The Lies and the Liars Who Tell Them

Once I started reading the chapters, I realized that I have heard this all before—old lie, new liar; new lie, old liar. So I built a matrix of the lies and the people who told them (Figure 11-1).

Figure 11-1. Lies and Liars Matrix

	Old Lie	New Lie
Old Liar		
New Liar		

I operated under the impression that, since 2006, some new lies and new liars had appeared on the scene, but others had persisted over time, with some interesting twists and turns.

I based this approach on an experience from almost 15 years ago, when I attended a learning technology conference after having been away from these conferences for about seven years. I'm not sure what I expected, but I found that the same people (literally) were making the same presentations (figuratively) with the same outrageous claims. All that was new were the technologies being touted and the scale of the claims. The presenters used powerful, seductive (to a learning audience, anyway) words and phrases like *revolutionize, dramatically increase,* and *significantly reduce.* And just as they had been seven years earlier, most of the claims proved to be false. They were nothing more than a figment of very creative imaginations, claiming as truth the often outlandish hypotheses that product marketers develop. Yet year after year we listened, and even all these years later it appears that we still do.

As I tried to fill in the matrix, I found that it didn't really work as well as I had hoped. I discovered that almost every new lie is some variation of an older lie. Sure, there are updates, upgrades, and refinements. But in the same way that cars haven't really changed all that much over time (four wheels, motor, transmission, seats), the new lies are just upgrades of the old ones. I kept looking for, but never found, the Tesla of lies about learning. There was no real game-changing technology, no radical departure from previous practice, no previously unheard of approach or solution. Instead, there is simply more of the same, just more creative and more interesting.

And as it turns out, the liars haven't really changed all that much either. Most, though by no means all, are vendors, analysts, pundits, and consultants—those who stand to benefit from buyers who believe their claims. I don't blame them; they all have jobs to do. I just wish consumers would demand more real proof of their claims. So with similar lies and the same liars, my matrix turned out to be more like a single cell, which hardly seemed worthy of a final chapter. So I started again.

Back to the Source

In the preface to *Lies About Learning*, I attempted to explain what motivates us to live with and accept the lies. I said:

> Why do learning professionals do this? Everyone is on a quest for the holy grail of learning—the one product, process, program, or promise that will allow them to dramatically improve the quantity, quality, and impact of learning in their respective organizations and to do this faster and cheaper than ever before. Because of this intense desire, learning professionals are willing to believe almost anything; they willingly, even enthusiastically, fall victim to some or all of the lies about learning. (Israelite 2006, vii)

Based on this passage, I've decided to take a different approach to the final chapter—one based on the perspective of the community of learning professionals who spend each and every day trying to deliver high-value, high-impact learning solutions to their customers. So as I thought about this quote and reviewed the content of *Lies About Learning* and this new book, I started to see a pattern. I saw two types of lies: lies we tell ourselves and the lies others tell us. While interesting, the lies others tell us are addressed elsewhere in this book. I'll focus here on the lies we tell ourselves.

Lies We Tell Ourselves

The lies we tell ourselves are the things we think silently to refute our doubts about what we are doing and why. In many ways, these lies are what allow us to make the expedient decision when we should know better, to implement methodologies absent evidence that they will work, or to take shortcuts we know we shouldn't. We might think of them as the little white lies we tell ourselves that help get us through the day.

Are they harmful? That's hard to say. But do they sometimes take us on detours that reduce the impact or value of the solutions we are trying to deliver? I am reasonably certain that this is the case.

I expect that the most common lie we tell ourselves is the learning equivalent of "I can name that song in three notes." A learning professional might phrase it as "I can help you reach your objectives in [some amount of time]," with the amount of time being considerably less than what we know we really need. In fact, the measure might not be time; it might be money, a delivery technology, or some other request. Regardless, far too often we talk ourselves into believing that learning effectiveness is somehow unrelated to the constraints under which we are asked to develop a solution.

Why do we do this? We fear that if we don't agree to unreasonable demands we will be viewed as being out of touch, unrealistic, not focused on the business, insensitive to the needs of our customers, or some combination. So what can we do about it? Well, that's a little more difficult. But allow me to suggest that earning credibility is the best place to start.

The story I used to tell about this issue is quite simple. Learning professionals often get requests for time management training or some other equivalent. We know that delivering a one-day program will rarely solve the problem, which our clients are often hesitant to even discuss. The first time I would get such as request I would deliver the program, making sure that it was well designed, delivered flawlessly, and well liked by participants. I also would make every attempt to set appropriate expectations. If the program went well, I would usually get another request, and I would fulfill that one too. By this point, I had developed a good relationship with my client, who viewed me as a credible partner who tried hard to meet her needs. So when the third request came, I would push back, suggesting that the solution isn't solving the problem, and engage in the kind of diagnostic that I had wanted from the start. But I had to be patient because credibility takes time. We have to earn the right to question our clients by delivering successfully on early requests, even if we know the solutions aren't optimal.

In the end, earning the trust of clients by delivering a few things they ask for (but may not really need) can open the door to truth-telling. It may not be as simple as telling them a particular program won't solve the problem. But it may allow for pushing back on or adjusting all sorts of crazy expectations, including the amount of time required to achieve a specific outcome, the budget to do so, the technology to be used, or some other cockamamie request.

Well, when I first re-read these past few paragraphs, I wondered: "Is my little story about credibility and trust nothing more than a little lie I tell myself?" That scared me, and sadly, I expect that the answer may be yes. But I do know that the technique has worked for me. And while it may not work as well as it once did, at least for a while I had found a small weapon to combat a much larger problem.

So what do we do about the lies we tell ourselves? Most important is simply acknowledging that we have a problem. We have less time, less money, fewer resources, and a greater sense of urgency than ever before. And our clients are experiencing the same things. They may also have unreasonable faith in our ability to deliver value, which tempts us to succumb to the pressure.

When you are forced (or willingly agree) to name that proverbial tune in three notes, jot down how many notes you really think it should take and why. Then plan how to get there in three notes. Look for opportunities to retrofit your ideas to fit your current context. Find compromises that aren't sacrifices. Dig for hidden opportunities.

Here's an example. My wife and I have designed a few kitchens, and our budgets are always lower than our desires. But that hasn't stopped us from looking at really high-end stuff—cabinets, appliances, lights, tile. While we couldn't afford it, this act of looking gave us ideas that we could apply as we designed within our budget constraints.

As learning professionals, we should always think a little bigger than we can afford. Just because we agreed to deliver a product within a set of unreasonable constraints (the lie we told ourselves), doesn't mean we can't think about what we might have done without the constraints. This serves as a reminder of what is possible, and far more important, prevents us from falling victim to the learning version of the Stockholm syndrome—we lie to ourselves with such strength and conviction that we actually start to believe the things we are saying. And that is when the real trouble begins.

Some Truths

To this point, I've covered the lies and the liars who tell them and the lies we tell ourselves. So I asked myself, where do I go from here? The answer was to go back to the title of the book.

The challenge with a title that includes the word "lies" is that it sounds negative. But in this case, the title was more a deliberate intent to amuse. In fact, it makes most people smile, hopefully because it contains an element of truth. Our profession, perhaps neither more nor less than others, has a propensity for telling its share of whoppers.

But remember there are also some truths about learning. And in many ways, they are more important than the lies.

It's About the Learner (Most of the Time)

One of our biggest challenges is figuring out who our customer really is. Very early in my career I worked on a government research and development project for which we developed almost 250 hours of training for M-1 Abrams tank mechanics. Our program had a sponsor, a funder, a buyer, an implementer, and a learner—five different stakeholders, all with very different agendas. Thus our meetings were full of jockeying for position and political arguments, but hardly any discussion of the actual learning experience.

Fast forward a few years. I developed a classroom program on project management for a very demanding customer. One of the explicit requests was to include a detailed module on budgeting, as this had been identified as a point of failure on many projects. I talked with the instructor after the first official delivery of the program (we had piloted it several times), and he told me he had gotten a lot of push back from class participants about the budgeting module, so he had decided to skip it. A vigorous discussion ensued. The instructor argued that his learners were his customers and, as such, should be able to influence what content they learn. I countered by insisting that the sponsor was the customer and had the right to decide what content the instructor covers.

Sometimes, we are beholden to the politics of learning. We have to deal with and, far too often, resolve competing agendas from the broad range of stakeholders who (attempt to) influence our work. How do we do our jobs when this occurs? I think the answer is relatively easy, although acting on it may be less so.

Almost any learning solution comprises goals, content, and design. The first two items are the exclusive domain of stakeholders, sponsors, and funders. But the design—the actual experience of the solution—should be focused completely on the learner. We should not let the politics of learning dictate how we create the experience of learning.

Design Matters

Several years ago I wrote about feeling like I was constantly listening to my own obituary. At conference after conference the speakers—often keynoters—proclaimed that instructional design was dead, that the field was completely irrelevant and the people who practiced it had become the learning equivalent of dinosaurs. As a proud, card-carrying member of the profession, I was a little shocked.

Had I more fully developed the earlier section on liars and the lies they tell, this lie would have fallen into the old lie/new liar quadrant. It seems that each time a new technology appeared on the scene, instructional designers were no longer needed because people from other professions would play their roles. Table 11-1 presents a partial list.

Table 11-1. Technologies and the "Fading" Role of Instructional Designers

Technology	The Role of Designer Is Played by
IBM PC (for computer-assisted instruction)	School teachers
Multimedia CD-ROM	Video producers
Learning games	Game developers
Web-based learning	Web developers and graphic designers
Webinars	Anyone with a keyboard and headset

In each case, after many—sometimes highly visible—failures, we found out that there was something to this instructional design stuff. It wasn't just about the technology. Some understanding about how people learn, the affordances that technology provides, and visual design were needed to create learning experiences that actually resulted in learning (a persisting change in human performance or performance potential). Go figure.

But to be clear, we are not a profession without our share of challenges. We need to become better partners and more businesslike in our approach to performance issues. We need to adapt better to the constraints under which our clients work. And, most important, we need to become better learners.

All of that said, I'm pleased to say that I'm experiencing a lull in the threats of my imminent demise. It seems as though we may even be seeing a little instructional design renaissance. And this is good, because design really does matter.

Methods and Tools Are Methods and Tools

In the early 1980s, Robert Reiser and Robert Gagné, professors at Florida State University, wrote *Selecting Media for Instruction*. They start the first chapter with:

For a good many years, educators and trainers have faced the problem of choosing the appropriate media to deliver an instructional message. However important may be the personal contribution of teachers, instruction as a totality is bound to be composed of one or another type of media. Educators and trainers throughout the world spend a great deal of time and effort in attempting to choose appropriate media for particular instructional situations. (Reiser and Gagné 1983, 3)

They go on to present a model and a method for assessing instructional situations and then systematically selecting the media best suited for helping learners achieve the instructional goals. Remember, this was 1983. The available options were limited by today's standard.

One of their major points is that instructional media are a means, not an end. There are days when I think that we have forgotten this important message. How often have we started a conversation by naming the delivery system before fully understanding the problem, analyzing the content and the learner, and writing the first objective? I have many times. And it has become a chronic problem in our profession.

In several chapters of *Lies About Learning* and of this book, contributors discuss how we have started to view new technologies as solutions in and of themselves, rather than as new methods or tools. We skip over the media selection process altogether. I'm guilty of doing this. But let's unpack this issue a little.

Could it be that a book on media selection in 2015 would focus less on the media and more on the instructional techniques that designers can deploy within the media to facilitate learning? Is it appropriate to view e-learning in the same way that we viewed a filmstrip 30 years ago? I think they are good questions, and honestly, I'm not sure of the answers.

But I do know one thing. The cycle of failure described in chapter 10 (Figure 10-1) is a direct reflection of the problem I raise here. If we adopt instructional media without weighing their characteristics (affordances) and the instructional problems they can solve, we are making a very costly mistake. We are thus saying that the medium is the (learning) method, rather than one of many tools the designer deploys to reach an instructional goal.

Methods and tools are just that. They are not solutions. Whether we use a modern version of the Reiser–Gagné model or some other approach to select the ways in which we solve a learning problem is largely irrelevant. But we ought to have a method.

A Few Final Words

I ended the first edition with the following:

> From ourselves we must demand more rigor. We must work harder to uncover the truths about learning that will free us to make the contributions we all want to make, that our clients expect us to make, and that, deep within ourselves, we know we are capable of making. (Israelite 2006, 214)

That pretty well sums it up.

References

Israelite, L. 2006. *Lies About Learning: Leading Executives Separate Truth From Fiction in a $100 Billion Industry.* Alexandria, VA: ASTD Press.

Reiser, R.A., and R.M. Gagné. 1983. *Selecting Media for Instruction.* Englewood Cliffs, NJ: Educational Technology Publications.

About the Editor and Contributors

The Editor

Larry Israelite

Larry Israelite was born and raised on a small chicken farm in Upper Black Eddy, Pennsylvania. Since moving to the big city, he has spent more than 30 years trying to answer the question, how can we improve business results through learning?

Currently, he is the senior vice president of assessment solutions at Smarterer, a Boston-based startup that provides testing technology to quantify skills and inform professional opportunities. At Smarterer, he is responsible for developing a comprehensive library of assessments that helps current or aspiring professionals make better decisions about their interests, capabilities, and career opportunities. He has held senior learning and talent management positions at several large organizations, including Liberty Mutual Insurance, Pitney Bowes, John Hancock Financial Services, and Oxford Health Plans. He holds a bachelor's degree in theater from Washington College, as well as a master's degree in instructional media and a doctorate in educational technology from Arizona State University.

The Contributors

Michael W. Allen

Michael W. Allen, chairman and CEO of Allen Interactions and Allen Learning Technologies, has had a long and lauded career in e-learning. He has worked on IBM's Coursewriter system; directed research and development for Control Data Corporation's PLATO system; developed the Authorware software, one of the most successful authoring tools; and introduced ZebraZapps, the most advanced visual authoring and multiplatform publishing system. He has been recognized with prestigious career awards from ATD, Ellis Island, the eLearning Guild, and many other organizations. And he has authored eight books on effective e-learning, including the ATD bestseller *Leaving ADDIE for SAM* (ASTD Press 2012). He is an adjunct associate professor at the University of Minnesota Medical School. He holds a doctorate in educational psychology from the Ohio State University.

Tina Busch

Tina Busch is the director of human resources for Kimberly-Clark's Global CFO Organization, leading the end-to-end talent lifecycle through the human resources business partner and functional talent management teams. With more than 15 years of experience leading learning organizations and driving global talent initiatives, Busch's work centers on the passionate belief that people and their knowledge are an organization's most vital competitive advantage. She is based in Dallas, Texas, and holds a doctorate in human resource development from Texas A&M University.

Mindy Jackson

Melinda (Mindy) Jackson is an instructional designer at Enspire (www.enspire.com), an industry leader in custom learning and simulation development. She enjoys the challenge of designing learning experiences that inspire change and enable performance improvement. She has presented on the topics of games, simulations, and other interactive learning environments at such conferences as SXSW, Training, TechKnowledge, ISPI, and I/ITSE. She is published in books, journals, and magazines, including *E-Learning Magazine, On the Horizon, Journal of Educational Computing Research,* and *Lies About Learning* (ASTD Press 2006). She received a master's degree in instructional technology from the University of Texas at Austin.

Doug Lynch

Doug Lynch, the chief academic officer for CorpU, has been a leading thinker in corporate learning for almost 20 years. Before joining CorpU, he was the vice dean at the University of Pennsylvania Graduate School of Education and also served as a director for the Wharton School's Aresty Institute of Executive Education and as a senior fellow at the Fels Institute of Government. A frequent speaker at conferences around the world, he has published widely in both education innovation and work-based learning. He recently served as the chair of ATD's Public Policy Committee, spearheading its initiative Bridging the Skills Gap. In 2013, he was voted by Harvard Kennedy School's *EducationNext* one of the most important thinkers in education. He holds a doctorate and an MPhil in economics and education from Columbia University. He did doctoral work in evaluation at Arizona State University, where he also received a bachelor's degree in economics. In addition, he has a master's of business administration in international finance from New York University.

Elliott Masie

Elliott Masie is a leading researcher, analyst, thought leader, and futurist in the fields of learning, collaboration, and workforce effectiveness. He is the chair of The Learning CONSORTIUM, a coalition of 200 global companies focused on the future of learning and knowledge. In addition, he is the host of Learning 2015 and the CEO of The MASIE Center, a think tank focused on the intersection of learning, education, and technology. He serves as an adviser to major companies, government agencies, and educational institutions on the changing nature of learning and knowledge as a component of performance and readiness. Recognized as one of the first analysts to use the term *e-learning*, he has 30 years of experience as a vendor-neutral advocate and analyst of the knowledge field. He is the author of more than a dozen books, including *Big Learning Data* (ASTD Press 2013). He has served on a wide range of corporate and nonprofit boards, including Skidmore College, the Central Intelligence Agency University Board, and the FIRST Robotics Competition.

Annmarie Neal

Annmarie Neal is the former chief talent officer at Cisco Systems and First Data Corporation. She is also the founder of the Center of Leadership Innovation—a worldwide consulting firm that specializes in business innovation and transformation through leadership and organizational excellence. She brings more than 25 years of global experience consulting with business executives and senior leaders across a range of industries to her writing, speaking engagements, business management, and consultation. She is the author of the recently published book *Leading From the Edge: Global Executives Share Strategies for Success* (ASTD Press 2013).

Daniel Sonsino

Daniel Sonsino is the vice president of talent management, learning, and development at Polycom, where he is responsible for global talent acquisition and management. He has 23 years of human resources and talent expertise with such companies as Polycom, HP, Raytheon, Bank of America, Sun Microsystems, and others. His focus is on building individual, team, and organizational capabilities in global companies.

Terry Traut

Terence (Terry) Traut is the president and CEO of Entelechy, a training design and development company based in New Hampshire that creates customized performance solutions for companies throughout the world. He has more than 25 years of training and management experience, and he has worked with more than 50 of today's top leadership gurus, including Jack Welch, Warren Bennis, Marshall Goldsmith, Bill George, and John Kotter. He has designed, developed, and delivered hundreds of courses in the areas of management, sales, customer service, and training. And he has developed training in a variety of media, including web-based training, computer-based training, self-paced instruction, and classroom training. He holds a bachelor's degree in education from St. Cloud University in Minnesota and a master's degree in human services administration from Boston University. He has also completed all coursework for a doctorate in human development and education from Boston University.

Edward A. Trolley

Edward A. Trolley is widely recognized for having started the training outsourcing industry when he orchestrated the first comprehensive training outsourcing deal between DuPont and The Forum Corporation in 1993. After joining The Forum Corporation, he continued to advance this outsourcing concept with leading companies such as The Moore Corporation, NCR, Texas Instruments, KPMG Canada, SmithKline Beecham, and Irving Oil. He has orchestrated more comprehensive training outsourcing relationships than anyone on the planet. He is co-author of the book *Running Training Like a Business: Delivering Unmistakable Value* (Berrett-Koehler 1999). He is also a contributing author to two ATD books: *In Action: Building Learning Capability Through Outsourcing* (ASTD Press 2006) and *Lies About Learning* (ASTD Press 2006). He is a highly requested presenter at industry conferences, and has spoken at major events such as the ATD International Conference & Exposition, TechLearn, World Outsourcing Summit, HRO World Outsourcing Conference, and, most recently, Outsourcing Summit 2014 in India. His concepts and ideas have been included in hundreds of business publications around the globe.

David Vance

David Vance is executive director of the Center for Talent Reporting and co-author of *Talent Development Reporting Principles* (TDRp). He was president of Caterpillar University from 2001 to 2007, and was named

2006 Chief Learning Officer of the Year by *Chief Learning Officer* magazine. Caterpillar was named Corporate University of the Year in 2004 and ranked number one in the 2005 ASTD BEST Awards. He is the author of *The Business of Learning: How to Manage Corporate Training to Improve Your Bottom Line* (Poudre River Press 2010). He received a bachelor's degree in political science from the Massachusetts Institute of Technology in 1974, a master's degree in business administration from Indiana University South Bend in 1983, and a doctorate in economics from the University of Notre Dame in 1988. He teaches in the doctorate programs at Bellevue University and the University of Southern Mississippi, and he is also the lead independent director for State Farm Mutual Funds.

Index

D

Data
  collection of, 86
  feelings versus, 85–87
Data analytics, 43–45
Delegation, 72
Design. *See* Instructional design
Designer affordance, 134
Digital generation, 5–6
Direct costs, 61
Disraeli, Benjamin, 69
Drones, 145
Drucker, Peter, 84

E

E-learning
  benefits of, 120
  classroom learning and, 7, 151–153
  criticism of, 126
  design mistakes for, 127
  evaluation of, 127–128, 130
  as impersonal, 125–127
  individualizing of, 129
  instruction expense and, 120–121
  instructional design for, 120–125,
    130
  instructor-led learning versus,
    125–127
  learning pronouncements about,
    151–153
  misconceptions about, 130–131
  overview of, xvii–xviii, 119
  performance-sensitive branching
    capabilities of, 128
  pitfalls about, 130–131
  presentation of, in short segments,
    129, 131
  savings associated with, 120
Economy, v–vi

Effectiveness, v, 166
Embedded learning, 12–13
Embellishment, 26
Emotional capital, 88
Emotional intelligence, 19
Employees
  communication with, 73
  development of, 58
  reasons for leaving organization, 75
Ethnography, 86–87
Evaluating Training Programs, 159
Event-based leadership development,
    77
Evidence
  gathering of, 22, 30
  hierarchy of, 31–32
  "preponderance of evidence"
    standard, 33
  in rules of court, 33
  standards for evaluating, 33
Executive development programs, 10
Experts
  instructors as, 10–11
  learning from, 10–12

F

Feedback, 73, 76, 80, 114
Feelings, 85–87
"Fingertip learning," 157–158
Fixed costs, 60–61
Forecasting, 103
Forgetting curves, 38
Formal learning
  description of, 26, 39
  economic expenditures on, 54
  informal learning versus, 124
  managing of, 54–56
Frankenleaders, 78, 81

HOW TO PURCHASE ATD PRESS PUBLICATIONS

ATD Press publications are available worldwide in print and electronic format.

To place an order, please visit our online store: www.td.org/books.

Our publications are also available at select online and brick-and-mortar retailers.

Outside the United States, English-language ATD Press titles may be purchased through the following distributors:

United Kingdom, Continental Europe,
the Middle East, North Africa, Central Asia,
Australia, New Zealand, and Latin America
Eurospan Group
Phone: 44.1767.604.972
Fax: 44.1767.601.640
Email: eurospan@turpin-distribution.com
Website: www.eurospanbookstore.com

Asia
Cengage Learning Asia Pte. Ltd.
Phone: (65)6410-1200
Email: asia.info@cengage.com
Website: www.cengageasia.com

Nigeria
Paradise Bookshops
Phone: 08033075133
Email: paradisebookshops@gmail.com
Website: www.paradisebookshops.com

South Africa
Knowledge Resources
Phone: +27 (11) 706.6009
Fax: +27 (11) 706.1127
Email: sharon@knowres.co.za
Web: www.kr.co.za

For all other territories, customers may place their orders at the ATD online store: **www.td.org/books**.

021514S.62220